THEATRE WITHOUT BORDERS

THEATRE WITHOUT BORDERS

ROBERT ASTLE

Signature
EDITIONS

Book design by Doowah Design.
Cover photo: Yves Simard in Les Deux Mondes' production, *Terre promise*. Photo by Yves Dubé.

We acknowledge the financial assistance of The Manitoba Arts Council and The Canada Council for the Arts for our publishing program.

Printed and bound in Canada

National Library of Canada Cataloguing in Publication

Astle, Robert
Theatre without borders / Robert Astle.

ISBN 0-921833-78-4

1. Performance artists—Canada—Interviews. I. Title.
NX513.A1A88 2002 700'.92'271 C2002-904511-8

Signature Editions
P.O. Box 206, RPO Corydon, Winnipeg, MB R3M 3S7

for Maria Antonella

CONTENTS

Acknowledgements

I could not have completed this book without the help of many colleagues, and the list is long. The artists across the country who took the time for the interviews, Wayne Specht, Wendy Gorling, Ronnie Burkett, Leah Cherniak, Martha Ross, Harro Maskow, Robin Patterson, Dean Gilmour, Michele Smith, Daniel Meilleur, Yves Dagenais, Sherry Lee Hunter, Shelly Wallace, Mary Ellen MacLean, Christian Murray; their administrators and agents who I hounded for print copy and photographs; my readers Endre Farkas, Mindy Parfitt, David Gow, Antonella Pelizzari and Anisa Cameron; my assistant, Vilma Mydliar; and the translator for the interviews with Daniel Meilleur and Yves Dagenais, Katherine Liberovskaya. Many thanks to Ralph Allison for inviting me to teach at Concordia University, Kit Brennan and Sherry Bie, who thought this book was a terrific idea, and my students, who were the real inspiration. I want to thank my editor and Iron Lady of syntax, Karen Haughian, who said yes to this book. I'd also like to thank Gordon McCall, Artistic Director of the Centaur Theatre for giving me the luxury of time as Playwright-in-Residence to focus on my writing projects, including this book. And I'd like to specially thank Jan Henderson and Jan Miller. With these two colleagues, I spent ten years developing, creating and touring clown and mask-based work with Small Change Theatre.

I would also like to thank my parents, William and Dorothy Astle, who over the years have supported my creative life with great interest.

Robert Astle
Zoagli, Italy
July, 2002

FOREWORD

In 1999 I was asked to teach an advanced clowning course at Concordia University. As I began to prepare the course I went in search of materials which would provide the students with both historical background and contemporary information. Naturally, my first stop was the library. I was dismayed when my research yielded almost nothing on Canadian artists except for the occasional article in *The Canadian Theatre Review* and in old copies of *Jeu* and the now-defunct *Theatrum*. There were no book publications or even an attempt to collect information. As a theatre practitioner myself, I knew that there was an astonishing body of creative work out there; but judging by the dearth of material, it was going to disappear without any written or photographic record. I felt that the information gap which existed in this area of theatre needed to be addressed, not only for my own students, but for this whole next generation of theatre students.

In the absence of available published materials, I turned to alternative methods for gathering this information. I recalled that the Canada Council had commissioned writer and artistic director Kim Selody to prepare a report on the state of mime, clown and imagistic theatre in the 1990s. Selody had travelled coast to coast, interviewing actors, clowns, directors, jugglers and writers who were working on the scene. I had spoken with Selody when he was doing interviews, but I had never seen his final report. When I contacted the Canada Council for a copy of the report, however, they said they had never heard of it. Luckily, Selody still had a copy and was kind enough to send it to me. The report did give me a very useful list of colleagues still working as actor/creators, mask performers and puppeteers, but it was also rather disturbing—already at the time Selody had been putting together his report many companies had folded, and clowns and satirists were giving up the cause, with the great ones crossing over to TV or heading to the United States. "No wonder the country is falling apart," I thought, "the clowns are all leaving." Perhaps most disturbing, some of the wonderful teacher/mentors had prematurely passed away.

I came to the realization that a book needed to be written about the Canadian artists who have managed to continue creating and building this type of original, but often difficult to classify work—call it clown, mime, mask, or physical theatre, imagistic theatre, puppetry or new vaudeville—in spite of dwindling resources and a mostly ignorant mass media. Despite these obstacles, and despite their ongoing struggle for survival and visibility, the artists I spoke to had one thing in common: they are all tenacious in their continual search for the essential metaphor, gesture, text, even the essential joke. They are all inspiring, well-informed and politically alert theatre artists, who use humour as their weapon of choice.

Although a book like this is long overdue, I am the first to admit that it manages to represent only a fraction of the theatre artists in this field who have been performing, directing and touring for many years. My intention, however, was not to write a report that is the final word on all physical theatre creation and performance in Canada, but to present a cross-section of some of the eccentrics, absurdists, puppeteers, raconteurs and solo performance artists who never fail to surprise and entertain us with their physical comedy, satire and subversive humour.

In my interviews with these artists I wanted to address issues that would be interesting and useful for students of contemporary theatre. I wanted the artists to be able to speak about their process of work, about where and how they found training and early inspiration, about what their particular voice is, and if they taught, how their teaching informs their creative work.

These artists have laid the tracks for the next generation, but for many readers, including students of contemporary Canadian theatre, the interviews collected here may be a first-time introduction to these artists; they have long and established touring careers, but because they must tour to survive, ironically, they are often better known outside the country than in their own hometowns.

Their hectic touring schedules made it impossible to get this group into one room to talk shop. Instead, after an initial phone conversation with each artist or company, during which we tried to get some of the anecdotes, gossip and touring stories out of the way, I travelled to meet them on their home turf and taped individual or group interviews. So, despite the fact that my subjects are eccentrics, clowns and physical theatre performers, I will admit to having applied some science.

■ ■ ■

INTRODUCTION

"I can take any empty space and call it a bare stage. A man walks across this empty space whilst someone is watching and this is all that is needed for an act of theatre to be engaged."

—PETER BROOK, *THE EMPTY SPACE*

The simplicity of the image of an actor walking into an empty space may be poetically and theatrically intriguing—but the obvious question is, what will happen next? Theatre and performance are deeply ingrained into our consciousness, but we always begin at the same place: silence or point zero. What happens next is the real adventure. The silence is broken. The skill, ingenuity and playfulness of the actor startles us. The details and sharpness of text move us, the care and attention to character and emotion imprint the theatre upon us like no other performing art form.

The theatre artists profiled here often break down what is called the fourth wall, the fragile dividing space or border between the audience and the actors. As well, their creations have toured extensively outside our borders. On stages around the world, these Canadian artists have earned great respect for their inventive performing style, which has its roots in the ancient traditions of mime, mask, *bouffon*, clown, *commedia dell'arte* and Greek tragedy.

Gathered here are some of this country's finest theatre artists who are searching, questioning and always invigorating the Canadian theatre scene. Some, such as Ronnie Burkett, with his breathtakingly fragile and zany army of marionettes, perform solo. Others, such as Les Deux Mondes/Théâtre de la Marmaille found inspiration in the 1960s revolutionary experimental theatre scene and in collaborations with some of Quebec's best playwrights. Companies such as Theatre Columbus and Theatre Smith-Gilmour had their genesis in the great École Jacques Lecoq in Paris. Jest in Time, the Halifax quartet of actor/clowns, also credits another great teacher, American Tony Montanaro. Still others, such as Theatre Beyond Words, have invented a communication language all their own which utilizes the simplicity and beauty of larval masks. Another company, Axis Theatre, has gone to the roots of ancient physical comedy forms such as *commedia dell'arte*, which has been hugely successful in their productions such as *The Number 14.* Others have melded creation with teaching. Wendy Gorling, for example, who recently collaborated on the stage and film version of Morris Panych's *The Overcoat*, is also considered one of the finest teachers of physical comedy in the country. And Yves Dagenais, the great Québécois clown, who began as a humble street performer, a self-taught clown, is now an esteemed teacher of physical theatre and clown performance at the National Circus School, the National Theatre School and Université du Québec à Montréal.

All of the artists profiled here share a high level of virtuosity, communicating stories through imagery, allusion and metaphor, creating characters who fully engage the audience. They have found the magic that spills over the borders of theatre.

▪ ▪ ▪

THEATRE BEYOND WORDS

"Physical Theatre? Visual Theatre? New Vaudeville? Clown? In fact, the best description of Theatre Beyond Words is a theatre of inventors, and if we had been scientists we would be inventors."

—HARRO MASKOW AND ROBIN PATTERSON

Theatre Beyond Words—The Inventors

Harro Maskow is considered, along with his former colleague, Adrian Pecknold,[1] to be one of the founding fathers of the mime, mask, and clown physical theatre movement in Canada. It was this duo that introduced Canadian audiences to the art of mime in the late 1960s and 1970s. As The Canadian Mime Theatre they toured this new art form across Canada, performing mime vignettes (usually short comic and/or poetic sketches) and teaching workshops. It was under the direction of Pecknold that they also created the Canadian Mime School. Maskow and Pecknold taught and performed tirelessly, mentoring many artists, some of whom are still working today in the field: Sherry Lee Hunter, founder of Jest in Time Theatre in Halifax, Nova Scotia, Sherry Bie, director of acting, playwrighting, and directing at the National Theatre School of Canada in Montreal, Quebec, and Wayne Specht, artistic director of Axis Theatre, in Vancouver, British Columbia, to name a few. During the late 1970s, the company was at an apex in terms of touring and teaching, and many of the artists featured in this book either saw the Canadian Mime Theatre in its heyday, or took workshops with it. Mime was a hot new theatrical form, especially with the added influence of television performers such as Red Skelton, Shields and Yarnell, and Marcel Marceau, whose huge North American touring success created both an audience and an interest in mime. Adrian Pecknold and Harro Maskow rapidly built a company and mime theatre school capitalizing on the new interest in the form—they toured incessantly, taking their work around the globe. Maskow and Pecknold collected a troupe of artists that today are still an essential part of the company.

The Potato People, 1988.
Nancy Potato: Paulette Hallich, Poppa Potato: Terry Judd.

The company got into serious financial difficulty after the purchase of the Royal George Theatre at their home base of Niagara-on-the-Lake in the 1970s, which caused an artistic rift between Maskow and Pecknold. As Harro Maskow describes in his interview, the company was literally thrown into the street. But with the aid of several levels of government and the commitment of a team of artists and hungry presenters around the globe, they were able to quickly re-establish themselves under the company Theatre Beyond Words, and the rest, as they say, is history.

In its new incarnation, Theatre Beyond Words attracted a new breed of artists who were highly motivated and willing to push the boundaries of the original form—breaking out of the silent and more illusionary mime and exploring all forms of clown, mask and text. The company attracted artists such as Robin Patterson, who joined the company very early in her career, after attaining a degree in English literature on the West Coast.

1 Adrian Pecknold is considered one of the founders of physical theatre in Canada. His book *Mime: The Step Beyond Words* is a valuable tool.

With this new team of artists, Theatre Beyond Words struck theatrical gold with its creation of a remarkable series of mask plays, featuring the now-famous naïve larval masks for the Potato People. Patterson, along with Terry Judd, Harro Maskow, David Satterthwaite, Larry Lefebvre and Paulette Hallich, invented a whole new world of communication for stage presentations, with an endearing family of characters, including Nancy, Mamma and Papa Potato. The demand for Theatre Beyond Words' work around the globe is testimony to its ingenuity and its groundbreaking mask and clown work. The company is touring throughout Canada, and I was able to catch a performance of *Seven Potato More* in Montreal.

This family of characters is finding an entire new generation of fans and I'm sure that many of the adult audience members remember seeing the Potato People in their youth and are now bringing their children to see them. The Potato People has become the international calling card for Theatre Beyond Words, although, as Maskow points out, the company has created many "general audience shows" in parallel to its children's theatre work, pushing its own limits, looking to re-invent wordless expression, and redefine its work. The members of Theatre Beyond Words are the inventors and pioneering artists of physical theatre in Canada; they have inspired a wide range of artists from coast to coast, and provided a model for many other physical theatre companies. As I turn on the tape recorder, I'm reminded of the first time I saw Harro and Robin performing in Vancouver in 1981. The show was *More Good Reasons to Laugh*—and by all accounts their energy and commitment to the company and creation have not wavered one iota.

■ ■ ■

RA: Harro, it's terrific to finally meet you in person. You are obviously in great shape. Were you an athlete when you were young?

HM: Never. I was always the worst—on stage I give an illusion. I was always stiff. I like to walk and run…I was never even a dancer! When I was a kid everybody said, "You move like Ariel." In one show, I have to squeeze into a little composter, which I have converted into a robot. Nobody else can get into that thing. Anyway, I am full of cramps and hurting after I make that robot go, but nobody else can make it move, or fit in it. Even with some of my arthritis, rheumatism and so on…

RA: Let's talk a little about the history of your work, which is tied to the Canadian Mime Theatre and Theatre Beyond Words. Has the company always been based in Niagara-on-the-Lake?

HM: Well…yes, all through the time of the Canadian Mime Theatre, and Theatre Beyond Words, our main base was Niagara-on-the-Lake, but it kind of happened gradually. I joined the Canadian Mime Theatre in June 1969… Adrian Pecknold and I had studied together in Paris at L'École Jacques Lecoq. Adrian worked at Stratford, playing Lucky in Beckett[2]. He got a grant to study at Lecoq, but only for a short time. One year. I'm not sure. But it was Paris where we met.

RA: You are originally from Germany?

HM: I'm German of origin, born at the Baltic Sea in Pomerania and displaced after the war to Western Germany where I went to school, then high school, and studied fine arts at the fine arts academy in Hamburg, and finished that up because I was in the section for educators. I also had to take courses at the University of Hamburg to get my humanities degree.

RA: Then to Paris?

HM: Yes, well, I had a chance to get a grant for further study near the end of my academic career, and they sent me to Paris—just do it for a year…see how you feel…you can always come back… And then I got stuck, hooked.

2 Pecknold's Lucky was considered a definitive performance according to Michael Langham, the artistic director at Stratford at the time. Pecknold also played Poco for twenty years on CBC Television's *Mr. Dressup*.

RA: How did you find out about the Lecoq School?

HM: It was through connections within the field. I had some friends who said, "You know, Harro, you've picked the wrong profession. You should be in this new field, mime." I wasn't particularly interested in theatre. I was interested in telling stories, playing, "miming things," although I didn't know the meaning of that, and so on, and these people said this was this new art form. I had no idea. But more and more friends were virtually kneeling on me to go. I said, "No, you couldn't make a living out of that, that's ridiculous." But from my time in Paris, I never turned back.

RA: This must have been a very interesting time for you to leave Germany and go to France.

HM: Yes, it was a completely new experience. I lived there for the better part of three years and always I went back to Hamburg in between during vacations to work as a taxi driver to make some extra money, to support my car and lifestyle in Paris.

RA: Did Adrian come from Stratford, Ontario and then end up at Lecoq's school at the same time?

HM: I think it was during my second year that Adrian was there. We met and had a good relationship, savoured a lot of things together and so on. There was another friend of mine, Arne Zaslove, an American. We got along famously in Paris. He was also just there for a year studying on a Fulbright grant. We had a much closer relationship—we formed a company outside the school and started to get things moving. He finally had to go back home. But when he was leaving he said, "You should come to New York, and maybe we can start a company there." I said I had always wanted to go to America—which for me was always this other continent, somewhere. It proved more difficult than I expected. We tried back and forth, but nothing came of it. Then suddenly he wrote to me that he was in Montreal and teaching at the National Theatre School. And they had just moved there from New York. So I went to the Canadian Embassy and they asked me, "Why would you want to go to Canada?" I said, "Well, it's exciting, a new country for me, a new environment, and apparently they don't have this particular art form. It's not very well known, but in Europe they are already up to their ears in it. "

RA: Did you come with the intention of bringing training in this very particular art form to Canada and starting a company?

HM: Yes, but it wasn't easy. After I arrived, Arne got fed up with the politics of the National Theatre School and was invited by Duncan Ross, the American producer, author and critic, to go to Seattle. After Arne left they couldn't find a good replacement for him. Then one day a little search committee from the National Theatre School dropped in and they saw what I did and said they had problems with the English section and were looking for a teacher. Many people said, "Don't take the job. They will overwork you and pay you very little. You'll have to get involved in the politics." I took the job and was hired for the English section, then the French section lost its teacher, and they heard that my classes went well. Suddenly I was teaching both in the English and the French section at the National Theatre School. It was all very exciting but after one year I thought, oh God, I want to perform.

Well, shortly after that Adrian walked into my life again, and he came through Montreal with his show and said, "There is a chance we're going to start a new mime company in Niagara-on-the-Lake."

So in the summer of 1969, I joined Adrian. Our first season ended up artistically successful but financially... When we opened the company, we realized many of the company members were not ready, so half the programme was composed of Adrian's solos, and then we added some of my solos, and a few pieces we'd worked up between us, duos, and then the rest of the gang did a middle number, an opening number and a big chase at the end. By the end of the season they were all gone. We ended up in debt. The company disbanded.

RA: It sounds like it was a rocky start.

HM: Yes. Then in the second year, when the Canadian Mime Theatre became more established, we hired Jiri Stanislav, a strange character from Czechoslovakia, and Wayne Specht.[3] Wayne stayed with the company, riding the ups and downs...

3 Wayne Specht is the current artistic director of Axis Theatre.

RA: Tell me more about the Canadian Mime School, which was created at the same time.

HM: I didn't do too much at the school. I was already up to my ears with performing, and I was working more from the engineering point, the technical side, making complicated props. I also repaired the masks, and worked at putting together the sound tapes, so there really was no time for teaching. Terry Judd, who is married to Robin Patterson, was a student at the Canadian Mime School, and so was Sherry Bie.[4] Terry stayed with Robin and they finally married. Just when they were ready to begin a new life together, the Canadian Mime Theatre collapsed. Everybody was out on the street.

RA: Was it a financial collapse?

HM: It was a double whammy…it was an artistic conflict between basically Adrian and the rest of us. He wanted to run it more as his company… It was his child—his creation and he wanted to keep it. Adrian didn't believe very much in democracy in the artistic field. The split happened at a particularly bad time. We had just bought the Royal George Theatre in Niagara-on-the-Lake. It looked like such a wonderful project, but once we looked at the renovation…they throw the book at you. In no time at all, the company was in debt. The company, which had always been in the black, now had this huge debt. To pay for this investment, the Board of Directors wanted to shrink the

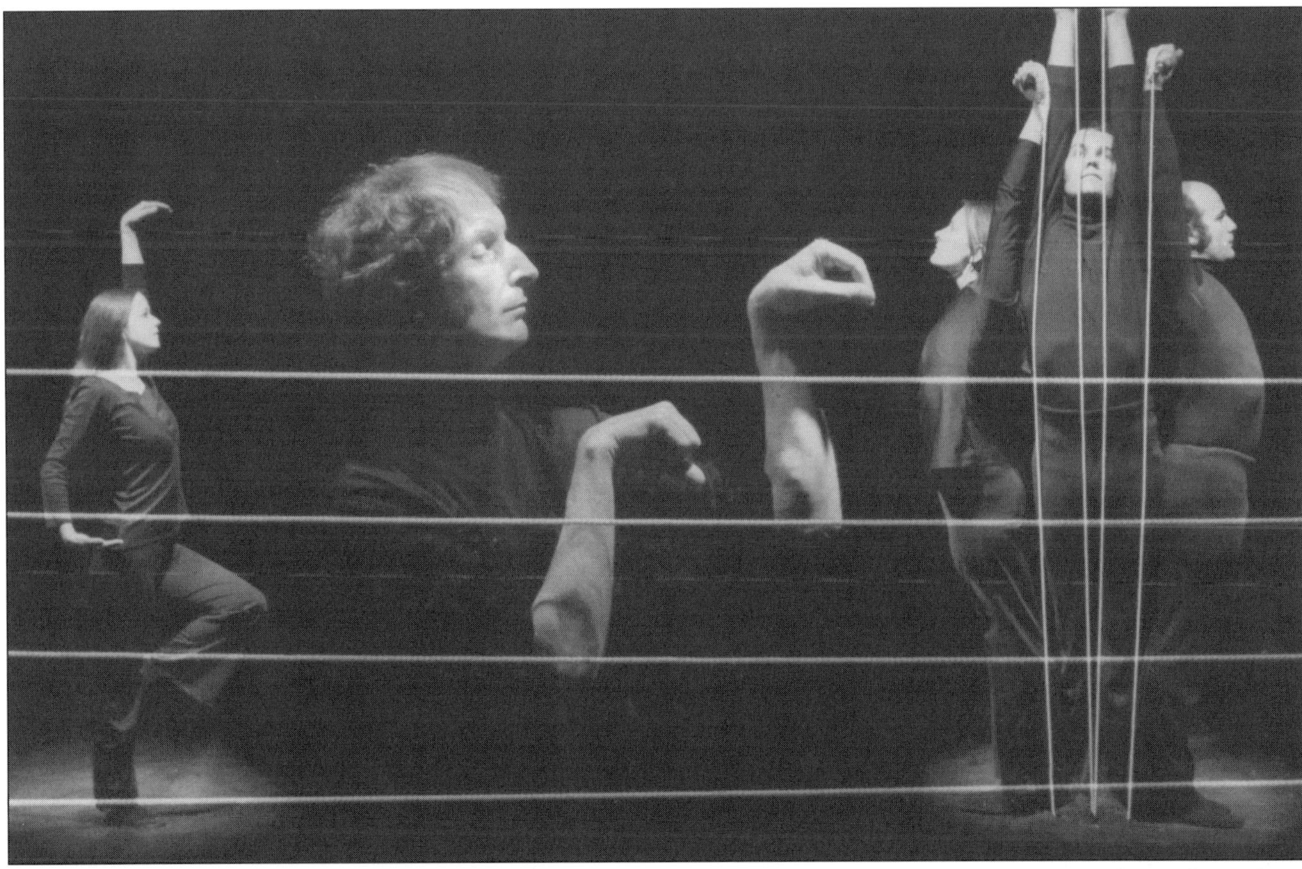

Overture, 1977. L-R: Paulette Hallich, Harro Maskow, Robin Patterson, Larry Lefebvre, Terry Judd. (Photo: Simeon Posen)

4 Sherry Bie, Director of Acting, Playwriting, and Directing at the National Theatre School of Canada.

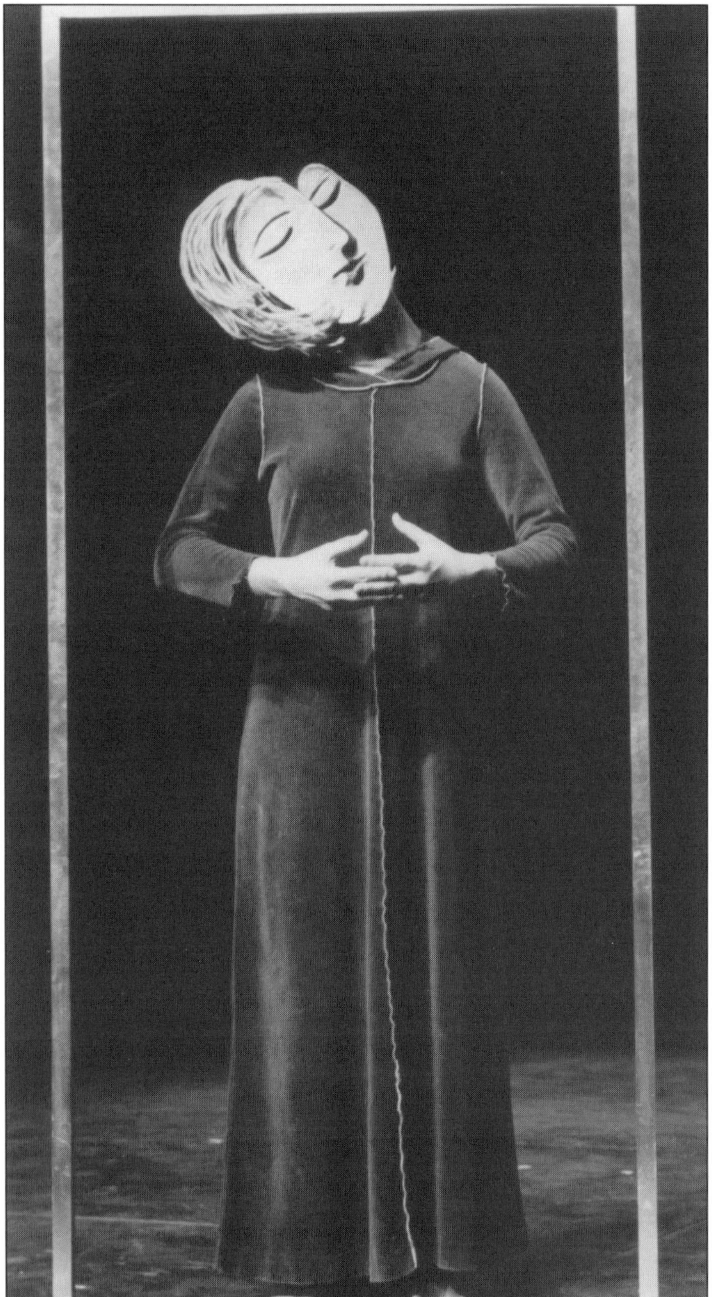

The Tourists, 1988. Picasso Mask: Christine Ribic.

performing company because they wanted every penny going into the Royal George Theatre project. When they asked us to cut back, from five actors to four and perhaps even three, that was the final conflict. It was sad. We were a team of actors for seven years and it fell apart with great acrimony. It was a hard blow for Adrian and caused a lot of bitter resentments from bank receiverships.

RA: So were there any winners out of this bad situation?

HM: The Shaw Festival was the lucky winner. The Shaw Festival needed a new space but couldn't afford it, but because the bank wanted to get rid of the Royal George, and the Festival had good support, it got a good deal, and was able to take it over.

RA: The formation of the Theatre Beyond Words Company was out of the ashes of Canadian Mime Theatre?

HM: Yes, and it was really ashes. We were literally out on the streets. Luckily, the masks were personal things, so we were able to hang on to those. The other thing we had was a network of sponsors all over Canada and the world. So, luckily, we were able to restart with some really important help from the Ontario Arts Council and the Canada Council. That was in 1977. You know, we worked like hell to prepare and rebuild a new company.

RA: Who were the artists who started Theatre Beyond Words?

HM: It was Robin Patterson, Terry Judd, Larry Lefebvre, Paulette Hallich, David Satterthwaite, who was our stage manager, designer, artistic everything, you name it, and me. We did everything, the administration, all of it.

RA: So, despite the collapse, you still had a desire to create and work. Is this really what keeps a group of such longevity together?

HM: That desire doesn't always last forever…it's like falling in love, and then keeping that up for a long rough life. That's the same thing there. So it's amazing what you can do when you have all this enthusiasm and energy. You do whatever it takes, and you can do amazing things…but then as the years go on, it's harder to find the energy and there is less enthusiasm…

RA: Harro, with the success of the Potato People, which is basically non-verbal, did you at the same time think about working with writers and text or spoken stories?

HM: We constantly made excursions with writers like James Reaney, John Lazarus, David Craig. They had a certain success, but of course, we were always at our strongest in the physical field.

At this point Robin Patterson joins in the conversation. She is also very busy with the day-to-day operations of running the company, and teaches various courses at Brock University and in Buffalo, New York.

RA: Robin, how did you get connected to this company, and particularly this field?

RP: I was at Simon Fraser University (SFU) studying English and Linguistics, but I also had a strong background in dance. Simon Fraser at the time did not have a professional theatre programme; everything like that was done extracurricular, so I did this on the side. There was also a wonderful woman working there, Mimi Baird. She programmed theatre companies to perform at SFU. She would bamboozle the groups into teaching workshops to the students for free. She would also throw a party and make them feel welcome, then ask them to give a workshop out of the goodness of their hearts…like it was their idea. She brought the Canadian Mime Theatre to Vancouver back in 1970, and that's when I met Adrian and Harro. I was very interested in mime.

RA: When did you finally join Theatre Beyond Words?

RP: I joined in the summer of 1971.

HM: She only spent a short time, but after she went through the Canadian Mime School course, Robin wanted more training, and then there was the girl part…

RP: I was a radical feminist, although I didn't particularly think of myself as a radical at the time. It was the early 1970s at Simon Fraser University; it was just what we did, or how we did it. John Juliani,[5] Peter Hyde[6] and R. Murray Schaffer[7] were all there. It was a pretty wild time. It was a pretty inter-connected place. There was incredible stimulation, so what I did, perhaps without really realizing it at the time, was to turn everything I was doing at university into something around theatre…I did the first individual studies at SFU, a whole semester creating, building my own work—if you can imagine, I had a chemistry professor, a psychology professor and a dance professor as advisors. It was self-directed. I had a strong sense of self-direction, so when it came to working with Theatre Beyond Words, I was really motivated, but I felt I did not have enough training. I had a very strong sense of self, of myself as a young woman, and I was pretty damned tough. So, I can tell you, when I walked into that scene at Canadian Mime Theatre…

RA: What scene was that?

HM: Well, at Canadian Mime Theatre, we were three men in the company, Adrian, Jiri, and myself, and one woman performing a minor role, so the idea of working with women was certainly new to us.

The Tourists, 1988.
Frank: Charles P. Schott

5 John Juliani, theatre and radio director and producer in Vancouver.
6 Peter Hyde, visual artist.
7 R. Murray Schaffer, composer and poet.

RP: I decided I was not taking anything like what I saw; the woman was wearing tights and leotards and the men wore pantsuits. Well, the 1970s were very "pantsuity," and I said: "If I am going to work with you, I am not going to stand out there in my underwear, while you are wearing clothes. I want to wear a pantsuit!" I ended up wearing the pantsuit. I basically told them, "I'm not going to hold cards and I want to create and perform solos!" I think I was pretty tough and demanding, but, you know, I also brought a lot of material, and they used that material for their next show.

Night Train to Foggy Bottom, 1990. Harro Maskow (sitting) and Melinda Little (Chest of Drawers) (Photo: Gordon Counsel)

RA: So that radical energy you brought to the company helped shape the future, then you survived the collapse and then the creation of Theatre Beyond Words?

RP: Yes. At the time there was Terry Judd, who is now my husband, and Sherry Bie at the Canadian Mime School. I went to Lecoq for further training from 1971 to 1973. That's where I met Ron East and Wendy Gorling. In fact, Wendy was at Simon Fraser at the same time I was.

RA: Robin, it seems that at a young age many artists weren't really thinking about the theatre as a profession, but then through either seeing the early tours of the Canadian Mime Theatre, or taking workshops, ended up in Paris, then caught the theatre bug at Lecoq. Would you say that it was like that for you?

RP: It is strange. I was planning on becoming an English professor. Anyway, I took my time, went to Europe for two years, then returned and have been with the company ever since.

RA: After all these years developing the Potato People and your particular style of theatre, where do you see Theatre Beyond Words in the Canadian theatre milieu?

RP: For many years, we didn't feel at all part of the theatre milieu. We were really on the fringe. It wasn't until we had more students and younger audiences that I realized that in fact we really are a strong part of the fabric. We really do bring different ideas and we think differently about collective creation. But, I guess it's our audiences across the country and around the world that endorse this idea of Canadian theatre. I'll admit that it's been difficult. We have always had difficulty defining the kind of theatre that we do. Is it physical theatre? Is it visual theatre? Is it new vaudeville? Or is it European clown? In fact, the best description is that it is a theatre company of inventors. If we had been scientists, we would have been inventors. And I think of a lot what we do is just coming into vogue now. For instance, the Shaw Festival is starting to use masks in their productions, which was a pretty radical idea even five years ago.

RA: So, you see your influence in theatre production, performance and design.

RP: Yes, but it takes time for ideas to become influential. The physical training and skills become critical to shape a complete actor, not just interpretation of text, but this influence is certainly evident on the Canadian stages in terms of physical actor training.

RA: So teaching is an important part of your vision?

RP: I only teach to learn to articulate what it is I'm thinking. I also think that now Jacques Lecoq is gone, it's up to us to mentor and teach, but in our own voices. We do have to reflect, because each one of us has endured.

RA: You created this physical style of theatre as inventors and have toured the entire planet with great success. Now where do you see the future of the company—through training and mentorship?

RP: We are working now with the deaf and hard-of-hearing community. We have just received funding for a research grant to bring these communities into our work and to ask them about their perceptions. It's fascinating. So instead of getting into institutional models, we are looking into communication, specifically non-verbal communication. That's something that we feel is really important. It's not a philosophical discussion, but more hands-on, person-to-person, trigger-to-trigger, looking carefully at body language and signals.

RA: Do you have any advice for young artists on how to keep and build an artistic group?

RP: I think it's because we've insisted on the collective creation right from the inception of Theatre Beyond Words. So that's our hallmark, as well as our work with the larval masks, which inspired us to create the characters, Nancy Potato, Papa Potato and Mama Potato. Obviously, to survive you need new input, but to work as a collective takes a ton of energy, humility and a sense of humour. I guess the sense of humour is most important.

■ ■ ■

The Golfers, 1977. Harro Maskow in three poses. (Photo: Stephen Fine)

1978. Paulette Hallich, Harro Maskow, Larry Lefebvre, Terry Judd, Robin Patterson.

PRODUCTION HISTORY OF
THEATRE BEYOND WORDS

POTATO PEOPLE SERIES

1999 **Spud Trek**
Conceived by Terry Judd, Robin Patterson

1997-98 **Rhythm and Shoes**
Conceived by Mike Peterson

1995 **School Daze**
Conceived by Terry Judd, Robin Patterson

1993 **Family Tree**
Conceived by Terry Judd, Robin Patterson

1991 **Survive the Great Outdoors**
Conceived by Terry Judd, Robin Patterson

1989 **Suite Potato**
Conceived by Robin Patterson
Music: Raffi Armenian

1988 **Seven Potato More**
Conceived by Robin Patterson

1986 **Double Play**
Conceived by Robin Patterson

1984 **Another Bag of Potatoes**
Collective creation

1981-82 **Uncle Clarence's Visit**
Collective creation

1979 **The Piggybank Caper**
Collective creation

1977 **Nuthin' But Trouble**
Collective creation

GENERAL AUDIENCE SHOWS

1999 **Off the Edge**
Collective creation

1997 **Still Laughing**
Collective creation

1991 **The Boy Who Could Sing Pictures**
Written by John Lazarus

1990 **Night Train to Foggy Bottom**
Collective creation with Coad Canada Puppets

1989 **Offensive Lines**
Written by David Craig

1988 **Babylon and Back**
Written by Michael Turner

1986 **West Coast Tempest**
Collective creation with Paul Thompson

1985 **Tourists**
Conceived by Terry Judd

1984 **Rites of Spring: A Clown Ballet for Lovers**
Collective creation with Theatre Smith-Gilmour

1981 **SOS**
Written by David Craig

1981 **More Good Reasons to laugh**
Collective creation

1980 **Traps**
Written by James Reaney

1977 **Five Good Reasons to Laugh**
Collective creation

LES DEUX MONDES

"I always say that if I were the prime minister of this country, I'd invent a universal social law that would oblige everyone to go on a trip, one trip to somewhere in the world, outside of their own country. Some time after the age of eighteen, get out and see the world. Because when you see it for real, when you feel it, when you touch, look, talk, communicate, you get a different understanding of humanity. You grasp the complexity of cultures, religions, and languages and the reasons, whether they be historical, or geographical, that determine certain behaviours and desires."

—DANIEL MEILLEUR, CO-ARTISTIC DIRECTOR, LES DEUX MONDES

Les Deux Mondes

Montreal-based Les Deux Mondes, formerly Théâtre de la Marmaille, is one of the great treasures of this nation. It champions collective creation, with a sharp-ear-to-the-world co-creation team that builds, writes, produces and tours total theatre experience for young people and adults around the globe. The company was formed in the early 1970s, inspired by the revolutionary and experimental theatre that was taking root in Quebec and Canada, which promoted the actor as author. It is known for its visually brilliant scenographies, combined with evocative soundscapes that underline stories such as *Umiak,* about the Inuit experience, the poetic and entirely wordless play*, Terre promise (Promised Land),* about the creation of the world, to *The Tale Of Teeka,* which is a harrowing reminder of generational violence and poverty in rural Quebec in the 1950s.

Umiak, The Collective Boat, 1982. François Camirand. (Photo: Paul-Émile Rioux)

The company's direction, passion and creative energy are directed primarily outward. Its vision is global, and nobody in this country has the international touring pedigree of Les Deux Mondes. Formed in 1973 by Monique Rioux and Daniel Meilleur, the company has transformed itself from being primarily a children's theatre company into one of the most respected theatre companies for both children and adults (or two worlds, hence the name Les Deux Mondes) in Canada. The globe is its playground, and its work is rigorous and challenging. It presents sometimes disturbing plays by some of Quebec's most outstanding authors, often in close collaboration with the core co-creators.

The company now has a team of three artistic co-directors: Daniel Meilleur, Monique Rioux and Michel Robidoux. This trio of artists has put together a formidable production company and built a state-of-the-art theatre laboratory in a *quartier défavorisé* in north Montréal. The work is flawless, and to witness a Deux Mondes production is to feel the power of total theatre—the image, text, character, action and emotion all running smoothly, coherently, like a perfectly tuned automobile.

Currently, Les Deux Mondes has over thirty people—artists and technicians—travelling all over the globe, in three completely separate shows, *Leitmotiv*, *The Tale of Teeka*, and *Mémoire vive*. At its home base, which is its laboratory, it has some twenty people working as a support staff or developing future projects.

The company has also collaborated on international projects. A particularly wonderful play called *Promised Land* (*Terre promise/Terra promesa)* was created with the Turin-based troupe Teatro dell'Angolo. The production, which has now been retired, was an elemental, universal play about the beginnings of the planet, to the modern era—told without a word spoken. All action was mimed in a contained space with the stage curtain drawn up about three feet from the stage floor, revealing a pile of dirt.

But the play that has really been embraced around the globe is *l'Histoire de l'oie (The Tale of Teeka*[1]*),* written in 1991 by playwright Michel Marc Bouchard. The play is haunting. In his opening notes the author describes it thus: "1955. Rural Quebec, caught between poverty and religious obscurantism. How were children raised in those days? With a stern eye, a firm grip, a wooden ruler and a leather strap. *The Tale of Teeka* is a story of laws."

Imagistically the play is flawless: two simple, stylized houses clad in metal are the central images—in the background a storm approaches. The environment is sparse—much like in an Alex Colville painting, where there is always a threat on the horizon. The central character is Maurice, a young boy living on a farm. Maurice is played by two actors, Maurice the younger, and Maurice the elder. The only other visible character is Teeka, a goose, and a puppet. The goose befriends Maurice, who almost certainly is a battered and abused child, left mainly to his own devices.

The sound score, created by Michel Robidoux, is a heart-piercing and integral part of the total experience. The exquisitely designed set is reminiscent of the "sacristy"—the religious ornamentation in rural Quebec churches. The main house opens to reveal the bathroom and bedroom of the little Maurice. Violence, abuse and rural life may sound bleak, but with stunning stagecraft and fine performances, this play really lifts us past the local and the colloquial and into the universal realm of theatre without borders. It is astonishing that while this work is almost operatic in scope, the entire work plays out in less than an hour.

I meet Daniel Meilleur in his office on a winter day in Montreal. Les Deux Mondes' work space and laboratory would be the envy of any Canadian theatre company. There is a roomy office above a large, well-equipped studio area, and plenty of space for storage, construction, and administration. The centre of this operation is the kitchen and dining hall, where the staff, artists and guests all gather for *la soupe.* The atmosphere is warm and convival. Daniel has just returned from Europe, where he was keeping tabs on his touring company.

■ ■ ■

RA: Daniel, first let me thank you for taking the time out of your phenomenally busy schedule. Where did you first get interested in theatre?

DM: I started in school, at the *cours classique*, which corresponds to high school. There was an amateur troupe in Thetford Mines, where I come from. So I did some theatre there. When I got to Montreal, I pursued cultural animation studies in university because I didn't know, coming from my region, that there were theatre schools. I didn't know that they existed.

RA: Was there a touring company or a particular show that made an impression on you?

DM: There was a troupe that made a really huge impression on me; it was "Le Grand Cirque Ordinaire." In the early 1970s they put on a show called *T'es pas tannée, Jeanne d'Arc? (Aren't You Fed Up, Joan of Arc?)*, which was a show that was very revealing, very revolutionary. It was about family, money, religion, love, everything. It corresponded exactly to my state of mind. So it really blew me away.

RA: How old were you?

DM: I was around eighteen. It was a real shock. And I thought that if theatre could do this to me, then I wanted to do theatre which could do this to others. Since then I've always had the feeling that at every show we give there's one person in the audience who transforms everything because they come to see me. It may sound a little pretentious, but the feeling is there.

RA: Where did you study?

DM: In Montreal, I studied at UQAM (Université du Québec à Montréal) in the cultural animation department for a year. Then the department divided into two sections: cultural animation and theatre. So I chose theatre. I didn't finish my studies. I did two-and-a-half years—I almost finished. But then the idea came up to form this theatre company with Monique Rioux, who was my teacher. So we did workshops with the Centre des Auteurs Dramatiques (CEAD) and we created a show. We came up with a name at the time: Le Théâtre de la Marmaille. We presented our show and we got good feedback. So I decided to continue to try to work with this company, telling myself that if ever it didn't work out, university would always be there if I wanted to go back. Of course, I never went back to university.

RA: Théâtre de la Marmaille initially came out of a university context?

DM: It might have been an age thing. We were young and we had the same ideas. Affinities developed. That's how it began.

RA: Was it always the company's intention to tour?

DM: From the beginning we wanted to be a touring company. We wanted to tour the world. That's what we wanted. But then we had to do it. You can't really just decide to go perform in New York. You can, but who pays? If you can pay, you can go anywhere in the world—like the Fringe Festival. So our goal for fifteen to twenty years has always been to invite theatre and festival directors to come and see us. Because they only invite you when they've seen you. If they haven't seen you, you don't exist. And it's very complicated to exist on the international scene. It's difficult, because competition is fierce. And people abroad don't bring in the kinds of theatre already being done in their country. If they invite a company, it's for something special: sensibility, originality, a form of expression they've never or seldom seen, or a show that's somehow exceptional from a national point of view. From the very beginning, from the 1970s, we did get some invitations, to Europe, first France…

RA: When did Michel Robidoux begin working with you as part of the core creative team?

DM: Michel came later than Monique and me. His first music composition with us was around 1976, but he wasn't the artistic director yet. He's only been the artistic director for the past ten years or so. By the way, next Monday, on the 28th of January, the company will be twenty-nine years old.

RA: Congratulations. Les Deux Mondes' work is very imagistic and visual, but you also work closely with writers. When you've toured your work outside of Quebec, to Canada and beyond, have you always translated the text?

DM: It sort of all happened from one show to the next. First, it's important to say that almost from the very beginning we've been translating our shows into English. That has definitely opened the doors to the rest of Canada for us. We've toured Canada coast to coast several times. We did it in the days when there was a circuit of youth festivals. There was one in Vancouver, one in Edmonton, one in Calgary, and another in Toronto. There also used to be one in Halifax. That's a circuit we did often. We often went to the Manitoba Theatre for Young People in Winnipeg. In Toronto we often went to the Milk Festival and to the du Maurier World Stage and the Young People's Theatre.

RA: Your theatre company is well known as a Theatre for Young Audience (TYA) company, but now with very sophisticated and challenging work, are you seeking more adult audiences? And do the shows still appeal to young audiences?

DM: In the beginning, we did only children's theatre. It's still the same principle. Last week the director of Cervantino, a big festival in Mexico, came to see us. It's actually the biggest festival of the Americas, North or South. It has a budget of $10 million US. It's a festival of the arts. There's two or three symphony orchestras and two or three big operas, operas from Europe, the US—huge productions. It includes dance, music and theatre. It is a very big and important festival. And the director, who didn't know our work, came to see us. Which is great, because we've wanted to go to Cervantino for years.

Crying to Laugh, 1980. Monique Rioux, Daniel Meilleur. (Photo: Paul-Emile Rioux)

RA: How do you manage to get all these marvellous invitations to the international touring scene?

DM: Getting the artistic directors of festivals to see our work is the only way. There is no other way. And the ones who know us well, who invite us, are the ones who are most strict. They come to see a show and if it doesn't interest them, they'll say, not this one… And among the people who know us, some prefer one certain type of theatre among the various types we do, and others prefer another type. Different people like different shows.

RA: What would you say are the real tangible benefits of taking your work beyond the borders of Canada?

DM: I always say that if I were the prime minister of this country, I'd invent a universal social law that would oblige everyone to go on a trip, one trip to somewhere in the world, outside of their own country. Some time after the age of eighteen, get out and see the world. Because when you see it for real, when you feel it, when you touch, look, talk, communicate, you get a different understanding of humanity. You grasp the complexity of cultures, religions, and languages, and the reasons, whether they be historical, or geographical, that determine certain behaviours and desires. When you see parts of the world where people won't let go of the geographic land their ancestors have lived on for centuries, when you're there, you understand, it becomes evident. It's a question of opening up and it's very inspiring.

RA: It must've been tough to create a demand for your work, because Canada was certainly not known as a theatre powerhouse.

DM: In the beginning, in the 1970s, the image of Canada was still very folkloric. And that's not that long ago. Only twenty-five years. It was an image of endless landscapes, forests, wooden houses, Eskimos, etc. So it was surprising to see a theatre from Canada that was contemporary, modern, avant-garde, political, activist, up to speed with the rest of the world. And in just a few years, in Montreal anyway—if you think of Robert Lepage, Denis Marleau,[8] Gilles Maheu[9]—theatre, and dance as well, have become an international attraction. At festivals, symposia, there are tons of people from here. When we do CINARS[10] and invite people here to Montreal, 200 people come from eighty countries. Because they know that in Montreal they'll see things that they won't see elsewhere. Why? I don't know.

I do know, though, that people imagine that there exists a formula to make an international show. We get told: "You have formulas to make it universal…" That's completely false. Take *L'Histoire de l'oie*. It's a little story from a remote part of Quebec in the 1950s. It's a show based on our childhood. When we talked about the show to theatre directors, they would tell us that there was enough about that on television and in the movies; it didn't interest them. And we were sure that we wouldn't tour the show, because no one was interested. And then little by little…because it was profound… To make something universal is like writing a novel that becomes universal because it speaks of very profound human truths.

RA: Can you speak about your process of developing your work?

DM: What's difficult with the creative process is that when I'm developing such-and-such a show, I'm not thinking about what a child will think or what the reaction will be, for example, in the States or Japan. I just think of a general public, because theatre is for the public, and the idea is to go as far as possible as an artist in the process…as far as possible… After that, every show has a destiny. Some of the shows we've created haven't worked. Some work, some don't. That's destiny. You can't explain why. It's mysterious.

RA: Is your work created collectively, that is to say, many voices working to create a whole?

DM: We do collective creations or collective productions. Now I just call it collective work. It's different because each artist "signs" the work, they sign the music, the video, the props, the directing, the actors sign, and everybody signs. Collective work is when you put forward your proposition and someone else suggests another and that's how you progress. It's not hierarchical; it's based on the idea that seems best, strongest. That's collective work. That's why our work takes so much time.

RA: With this process of collective work, as you describe it, how do you make decisions on holding on to the good ideas, and letting go of the bad, or not-so-good ideas?

DM: It's a long process. Within this process you keep holding on to your ideas. There are ideas you won't give up for the world. Because you believe in them! But sometimes, three or six months later when you're watching the video, you realize the problem lies in what you believed in most. You'll say: "The idea may be great, but not in this show." It's a distance you don't have when you're right in the action. You won't give ideas up when you're too close to them. So it's a process that leaves room for reflection, for some distance. When you're working on a show from morning to night, wherever you are, you're always thinking about it—when you're reading an article, or even watching a TV show. You're always thinking about it. That's very important.

RA: How long does it take to create a piece of theatre for Les Deux Mondes?

DM: From the idea to the show, it takes five years. But, in the first place, we're a research and development troupe. And we've always done pre-research projects. We try to never redo what we've already done. If you look at the shows that are playing now, *l'Histoire de l'oie, Leitmotiv* and *Mémoire vive*, it's three different universes. Someone who doesn't know us may not even imagine that the same company created the shows, because our research goes in such different directions.

RA: Do you always follow the same creative process, or has it evolved over the years?

DM: We are still working with the same process we worked with when we were younger. Then it was less articulated. But

8 Denis Marleau is the director of Theatre UBU and the National Arts Centre, Ottawa.
9 Gilles Maheau is the director of Carbone 14, Montreal.
10 CINARS (Commerce international des arts de la scène), held in Montreal every two years for buying and selling of touring attractions.

you'll notice that these shows are very different. Our early work had audience participation. *Umiak* is a beautiful show. There was a time—I don't know if you remember—when no one spoke of the Inuit. Inuit and First Nations stories were not popular subjects. I remember when we did that show. We still get requests for it. It has remained a very mythical show. We organized a sort of convention to re-examine it. We brought together people from the company and from outside and watched the video to see if it would still be relevant to do the show today. It was a thinking and reflection committee. We watched it and decided that we couldn't do that show today, because the situation has become politicized. Today there are important realities that would need to be integrated into the show. We had been inspired by mythology, where there were no contemporary elements, only very traditional stories.

RA: Are you talking about the issues of appropriation of voice and presentation of native cultures by non-natives?

DM: Now you have to work with certain subjects differently.

RA: Your organization is certainly substantial, thirty artists travelling the globe, and a major theatre laboratory space in Montreal. Do you find the work as satisfying as, say, when you were just starting up the company, facing all the challenges that entails?

DM: It's been a long battle, a lot of work, and it's still a lot of work today. Theatre is so fragile. If you do a show that doesn't work, the price to pay is huge because you've invested so much. The way we work enables us to stop projects in the middle. When we do a three-week workshop, everyone is paid, from actors to technicians. We work with props at hand, we quickly invent things, we listen, we look and sometimes we find that it's not interesting and we decide we don't want to continue. Then we stop, because we can stop and all we've spent is seven to eight thousand dollars and everyone has been paid. But if we feel there's something there, that is where it can become costly. It can cost $50,000-$100,000. And in the process you might know that it's not great, that it has problems. And you go ahead and do it and it fails with the public. Then you've lost the money, and there's nothing else to do with the show. You've just basically failed. Our method enables us to explore and to abandon research projects.

RA: Have you learned from failed experiments?

DM: We do this now because we've done otherwise. For example, we had advance contracts for new shows and we were part of a machine. We had to produce for a certain date because we had signed contracts. We've done that and it didn't work. Twice. So we said, "Never again will we do that." We decided that it's always the right time to put on a good show. And from then on we stopped working with getting into advance contracts. Otherwise you burn yourself out and it's very frustrating for the artists. Nobody wants to end up with a flop. Everyone wants to do something that works. But sometimes it doesn't work. Sometimes there are problems, not only in the concept but also with personalities. There are people who are in bad periods of their lives for personal, family, love, whatever reasons. You're in a process with someone who's not functioning. That's life. That's why we prefer the way we work. It also allows the artists the freedom to take a break. They're not obliged to do anything. They don't have to like everything. It's okay if they feel uncomfortable. They can have other things going on the side.

RA: The process is open—is that what you are saying?

DM: It is freedom, your freedom to invest yourself as much as you want and your freedom to leave if you want. So when we work with people at the beginning of a research project, it's not necessarily to end up with a show. It's to get through one stage of the research process. We also retain the freedom to say that we don't want to work with someone anymore. That's how it is.

RA: So, the investment of the artists' time is respected. But how do you deal with writers, who have perhaps a different investment?

DM: The way we work can make people very insecure. We're not afraid to throw away good ideas. It can be discouraging. We get somewhere and don't continue. It is a very tough process, tough for the authors, tough for the actors, tough for all the artists. Because you progress and when you reach an important stepping-stone, that changes everything. You have to let some things go. That's very tough.

RA: You collaborate with artists from various regions. For instance, you created *Promised Land* in collaboration with Teatro d'ell Angolo. How was that process?

DM: It took us three years to do *Terre promise* with the Italians. That was a magical collaboration, incredible.

RA: How did you find the vocabulary for writing *Promised Land*?

DM: First, we improvised. We were three Canadians and three Italians. We improvised in pairs. Sometimes we improvised in French, sometimes in French and English, sometimes in French, English and Italian. We improvised—we spoke. And when this curtain idea came up, all the words just vanished. But we found that through the research. It was during one of our meetings. There were nine meetings in all. That's what we started with. It was a good way to get to know each other. And the theme was always t*erre promise*—the promised land. So there were all sorts of scenarios, some in airports, and others where there were identity changes. Our improvisations came from the two other teams that each sent us one word. I remember that we were at the theatre in Italy, in their theatre, and the words were miniature, small. So we started to look around the theatre and we began to play with the curtains. And that's how we found that little scene. And then we just added the hand. And I remember calling Nino to see. Then we tried with arms, legs… We ran across the street to the hardware store to buy a bag of earth. We picked up rocks, whatnot, from outside. And that's how we started to play, to work. We had the beginning. But that was after a first meeting in Montreal. This was the second meeting.

RA: Did you begin working in Montreal, or in Italy?

DM: We started in Montreal. The second phase took place in Italy, then again Montreal, and Italy and the last here. It was developed during five stages in all.

RA: Was there a moment when you all went, "We now have the play"?

DM: I'll tell you more about *Terre promise* to explain what the research was about, what a theatre laboratory is. I compare myself to a scientist. So, we did the first part of the show. It lasted about fifteen to twenty minutes. We said great. But then the curtain would go up, and because that beginning was so strong, every time that curtain went up it was a catastrophe. So we improvised and improvised. We tried everything and I mean everything: prehistoric man and some really stupid stuff. We tried. We worked and worked and at some point we said, "let's string everything we have together and not stop, no matter what happens." So we do the first part. The curtain goes up. We go on with our stuff and more

Leitmotiv, 1997. Noëlla Huet and Martin Rouleau. (Photo: Yves Dubé)

or less by accident the curtain falls. But we had said that we wouldn't stop, so we continue. And then we notice everything going on when you don't see the actors' heads. It's all there. And the same stupid sketches with the curtain hiding the top of the actors' body became magnificent, huge, and universal... And it all came from a mistake, an error. Much like in science, in pharmacy, in chemistry, they often come across discoveries by accident, some freak phenomenon, and it's all there... and you verify and reverify and you realize that while you were looking for one thing, you found another. For this you need to have certain antennas and you need to recognize mistakes. I really like the freedom of playing around at work. We try out the most ridiculous ideas. When you're playing around sometimes you can find something completely surprising, which is not quite right but takes you somewhere. It's good not to censor yourself.

RA: So you really do trust your instincts, or at least you have developed strong instincts. Do you also let the actors become part of the creative work?

DM: That's the actor's revolution. In the twentieth century, the actor has become an author. That's what the twentieth century did for actors. As for myself, I go even further. My musician is an author. I consider him to be an author, and I consider the videographer to be an author. They are co-writers. The goal is first to write a show. Then we see if it holds together and can be produced. Is the music good for release on CD? Will the images last? History will decide.

RA: You must hire many young actors. What do you see lacking in the training actors receive?

DM: Young actors who come out of the National Theatre School need to be broken. Usually it takes three to four years to undo what they've learned at the school. But there is nothing like having rules to break. It's like dance: a dancer with solid classical training will be a good contemporary dancer because he has very rigorous techniques and a well-developed body. With that kind of baggage you can have fun. You can let go completely, because you have the technique.

RA: It must be a very difficult process to find actors who are willing to commit to working on the development of new work. Do they really understand what is being asked of them?

DM: When actors see our shows they want to be in this kind of show. But the process is very demanding. It can be extremely depressing and difficult because we're always working with the unknown, we're in the dark, we "hit walls," we can be blocked for weeks. This week, for example, there are eight people working and nothing is coming out of it. What's going on? It's very, very hard.

RA: Are courage and tenacity job requirements?

DM: It does take courage and tenacity. It also takes hope and, of course, a sense of humour. (And lots of beer.) Often it's when you go for a beer at five o'clock, after having workshopped all day, that the ideas come. When you're more open, you see things from a different perspective.

RA: Your company has an incredible history of building multi-award-winning plays, yet in Montreal, despite this international record, you are virtually unknown.

DM: The price to pay, as many others have already said, is that nobody is a prophet in their own country. There's a mentality here that if you leave home, if you don't want to stay with your parents, you're quickly forgotten. That's the price we pay, because we don't want to be part of the local scene. We're very integrated here, though; we do a lot of work in this neighbourhood. But our work is different. We've also never wanted to be part of the publicity machine, to advertise "the new show by Daniel Meilleur or Monique Rioux." We've never wanted to get into the name thing, like Maheu, Lepage; they don't work like we do. We've never wanted to do what they do. We even avoid doing interviews by ourselves. Because things come out in newspapers that make us angry, and we say, "I never said that," but the other says, "It's in there." So normally we propose to do interviews two of us at a time, but journalists often say that they don't do two at a time, so we just don't do the interview. That way we protect ourselves from the inside as well.

RA: Les Deux Mondes is a phenomenal success, in terms of any theatre company, children's or adult. It seems you are really the ne plus ultra of touring companies. With close to thirty people on the payroll around the globe, in three different shows, what is next for the company?

DM: Every theatre company has its destiny. We are what we are because of the work we've done. And it's hard to keep up with everything at once. In Montreal we send out two hundred press releases and in spite of that, for example, some newspapers never said a word about our last show, *Mémoire vive.* There were no reviews, nothing.

RA: Is it difficult to find an audience in your own backyard?

DM: We think it's too bad because we do perform a lot in the province of Quebec, a lot in Canada. And we do a great job now. We prepare the public. Sometimes in the theatre lobbies there are seventy-five volunteers doing theatre, sculpture, painting, song, on the themes of our show. Our shows have become events. It's done about a month or a month-and-a-half before we come. Like now in Ste-Geneviève, we've been working with the local people for about a month or a month-and-a-half for *L'Histoire de l'oie.* And the locals express their ideas about violence against animals, not necessarily against geese. When you come in, there may be a choir, music, sculptures, paintings, people performing different things, written stories... All this is before our show. And these seventy-five people are, of course, invited to the show. But

Mémoire vive, 2000. Catherine Archambault. (Photo: Yves Dubé)

these seventy-five people invite their brothers, sisters, uncles, aunts, wives and cousins, so we're always sold out. In rural Quebec we fill the theatre more than television stars do. But this type of work takes a lot of energy. So when you're working like that, you're not working with a publicity firm to get your picture in the paper. You're investing elsewhere.

RA: The name Les Deux Mondes certainly is synonymous with wonderful theatre, with meticulous imagery and text. What has been the response to your work in the United States?

DM: At SUNY Purchase, a university in the New York City area, the director invited all three of our shows in one season. That was his programming. Imagine that. We performed at the Santa Fe festival in the U.S. for three years in a row. The first year some 400-500 people came, the second 600-700 and the third over 900 people came to see the four shows. We have a public and we have a name. There are places that when you come back you fill the theatre because people talk about it—much more so than in Montreal. It's too bad, but that's the way it is.

RA: What are you developing now?

DM: We're working on a new show with Jacques Languirand, a Montreal radio personality. We've started to work on it. We were also working with the French writer, Michel Azama; I was disappointed with the second phase of the workshop, so I've put a hold on it.

RA: It must be a very tough process for authors as well, because of the ownership issues around text.

DM: It's difficult for authors to work with us because our shows are based not only on text. That's how *The Tale of Teeka* was written. The first phase of the work we did on that show could all fit on one page, but the musician was there, the set designer was there, as well as the actors and me. And this page—and later two pages, is what all our work came out of. But it was a team. Nobody would have come up with the work by himself or herself. Michel Marc Bouchard could not have written the text on his own. The music would not have been composed alone in a studio nor the set design imagined. It was the product of interaction, discussion, music that inspired images, images that inspired words, words, scenography. You have to let these things come…

RA: Normally companies of your size are asked to generate five shows a season, so how can you afford the time to work?

DM: The argument that we don't produce much… Those who produce two, three, four shows a year, how many times do they perform them? Thirty, thirty-five times, max. Whereas this season, for example, we're performing one hundred and twenty shows. That would be the equivalent of putting on three new shows. But instead of spending three times as much for three new productions, which would probably be quite average, with the shows that work well we reinvest the money we make touring into research, into work on new pieces. So it's touring that brings about new productions. And instead of counting on a certain number of new shows, we count on the number of performances to subsidize our work. Such calculations are debatable of course.

RA: Is it difficult to find actors who are willing to work away from home most of the time?

DM: The actors that we work with are into touring. Like the ones in *l'Histoire de l'oie*, they are really into it, and it's phenomenal. You don't run into people like that often in a lifetime. It's a phenomenal career. We went to Argentina just before all the events; there were demonstrations everywhere in the streets. It was quite an atmosphere. Now we're in Quebec to do a few shows. Then we're going to Brazil. Next year we're doing a huge tour of France. We're going to play at Palais de Chaillot in Paris. It's amazing. It doesn't stop. And the actors are totally into it. I watched the show again last week at the Saidye Bronfman Centre where the Maison de la Culture Côte-des-Neiges held *l'Histoire de l'oie* for the neighbourhood schools. It's always amazing to see the kids who come to the show. Something really powerful happens.

RA: Do you think that for young artists you have created a model for creation and international touring?

DM: Our dynamic is completely different from typical theatre production. The history of our company is very dynamic. And it works. But I can't say that I think it's a model necessarily for everyone. It has to do with our particular personalities, with chance events and meetings.

RA: Does the slow, long-term process of development work well for your company?

DM: That's how we work. That's the way of working we've invented and it takes courage. Also, because we tour a lot, there are moments—like before leaving for a tour or when you've just come back home—that are not good for creative development work. In reality, it doesn't leave much time for development work on new productions. So every year, if the show we produce is successful, which often happens, it involves a lot of touring; 120 shows in a year is huge. That doesn't leave much time for other work. But sometimes, like last year, we perform much less and then have a lot more time for working on new ideas. It's a lot like in dance. Édouard Lock[11] takes up to a year to prepare a show. And if it works, he tours the world for three years. That's his pattern: for a year he almost doesn't perform at all. He's doing research in his studio. Then he launches it and if it works well, it's a real world tour for La La La Human Steps. We're often compared to dance companies. So some years we perform less and develop more. For instance, our wonderful show *Terre promise* is now over, but we toured for eleven years. We had two complete teams for it. One was here, and another identical one was in Italy. So we often performed at the same time in two different countries. It was a great adventure. And *Terre promise* ended in Jerusalem, the promised land…our last show was in Jerusalem.

RA: What better place to let it go?

DM: I think that a show has a soul. And at some point the soul leaves. You can't explain it, but you can feel it.

▪ ▪ ▪

Promised Land, 1993. Yves Simard. (Photo: Yves Dubé)

11 Édouard Lock is the choreographer and artistic director of La La La Human Steps, based in Montreal.

EXCERPT FROM THE TALE OF TEEKA* L'HISTOIRE DE L'OIE

LES DEUX MONDES–MICHEL MARC BOUCHARD

Setting: late summer 1955. A farmhouse with its outbuildings, enclosed by a fence. An overall impression of austerity. A storm is brewing in the distance.

MAURICE (ADULT): Lightning struck not far from the house. Maurice felt that he had to be obeyed. Suddenly, he heard the voice begging him to come down from the roof. Frightened, he obeyed that voice.

Maurice (child) climbs down from the roof and disappears behind the house.

Only then did lightning strike, several times, on his head, his body and most of all his arms! For a fraction of a second, Maurice thought it was the thunderstorm... *(Beat).* It was not the thunderstorm. The anger of Bulamutumumo was fading in the distance. The sound of groundhogs, toads and sparrows could be heard once again.

Enter Teeka, a white goose puppet manipulated and played by Maurice (adult).

TEEKA: I loved thunderstorms. The sky released showers of earthworms, plump and ready to eat. And this time, they were all for me. It was one of the few advantages I found in my solitude. I lived in a very small house near Maurice's. Earlier that week, my house had suddenly become too big for me. I had watched all my fellow geese enter the barn...and I never saw them come out again.

(Observing an earthworm.) This one or that one? I'll turn the first one to move into a mere mouthful! He moved! Let's allow him to wriggle a bit longer, enjoy the few seconds he has left. A bit of play, in the name of sportsmanship! On your mark, gulp! *(She eats it.)*

My own mother had disappeared into the barn when I was only a gosling. That was the day I met Maurice. He brought me a handful of insects, dead and mutilated. I was touched by his gesture but tried to explain that this was not my usual fare. *(She honks.)* My voice frightened him. He dropped the poor butterflies that he had transformed back into caterpillars and fled. Another one moved! He obviously has no sense of danger! Innocent creature! Too much pity leads to famine. Gulp! *(She eats the worm.)*

The following day, I decided to adopt a more tamable attitude. This time, Maurice offered me some grain...I allowed myself to be tempted...it wasn't the delectable grain my fellow geese had ingurgitated several days before disappearing into the barn, but it was tastier than what they usually made me eat. *(She honks.)* My voice frightened him again.

I realize the song of the white goose is much less melodious than that of the swallow or even the chirping of sparrows, which I personally find unbearable.

Yes, in some countries we replace watchdogs and we honk at the slightest sign of danger. Remember the Geese on Capitoline Hill! Yes, it was my ancestors who alerted the sleeping Romans upon the arrival of the invader. We are very proud of this historical exploit and the story is transmitted from gander to egg.

And another one who dared move! Unfortunately for them, earthworms don't honk! Such a pity! Gulp! *(She eats the earthworm.)*

Maurice came back for the third day in a row. It was his turn to frighten me. As I was allowing him to pat my neck, he began to tear out some feathers. I am not an ant, nor a butterfly… I bit him…

That is how we tamed our solitudes. *(To the earthworms.)* Their sluggishness exasperates me! Gulp!

My long days were filled with the memory of my fellow geese and our conversations about tomorrow's weather, about different grooming techniques and stories of our glorious past. But I had discovered another pastime: observing Maurice.

> *Maurice (child) finally comes out of the house. His arm is in a sling.*

■ ■ ■

The Tale of Teeka, 1993. Maurice child: Yves Dagenais, Maurice adult: Alain Fournier (Photo: Rabanus)

* Reprinted with the permission of the author, Michel Marc Bouchard, the translator, Linda Gaboriau, and the publisher, Talon Books.

PRODUCTION HISTORY OF
LES DEUX MONDES & THÉÂTRE DE LA MARMAILLE

2001 **Mémoire vive**
By Normand Canac-Marquis and Daniel Meilleur
Translated into English by Linda Gaboriau as *Living Memory*
Winner of Les Masques Awards (2002) for Special Contribution to Theatre.

1996 **Leitmotiv**
By Michel Robidoux.
Translated into English by Linda Gaboriau and into Spanish by Gilberto Flores Patio.
Winner of Les Masques Awards (1998) for Special Contribution to Theatre and Les Masques nomination for Best Sound Environment.

1995 **Rosemonde**
By Louis-Dominique Lavigne; Original idea and interpretation: Monique Rioux;
Published by Lanctôt Éditeur (1996). Translated into English by Mark Bromilow as *Rosemonde.*

1994 **Les nuages de terre**
By Daniel Danis.
A co-creation with the Ki-Yi M'Bock Theater, Abidjan, Ivory Coast. A co-production with Le Centre National des Écritures du Spectacle (La Chartreuse) (France), La Fédération des Amis du Théâtre Populaire (FATP), Festival International des Francophonies e Limousin (France), Espace des Arts de Chalon-sur-Saône (France), Festival de théâtre des Amérique (Québec).

1991 **L'Histoire de l'oie**
by Michel Marc Bouchard.
Co-production with the National Arts Centre. Published by Éditions Leméac (1991). Translated into English by Linda Gaboriau as *The Tale of Teeka*, into Spanish by Gilberto Flores Patino as *La Historia de la oca.* and into German by Marie-Elisabeth Morf as *Die Geschichte von Teeka* . Awards include: Best Fiction Award from Le Gala du Livre (1991) du Saguenay; Best Production awarded by Le Conseil des arts de la Communauté urbaine de Montréal (1991); Best play created for the stage (1991-1992 season) awarded by the Quebec Theatre Critics Association; Best Foreign Theatre Production (1992) awarded by La Union de Criticos Y cronistas de Teatro de Mexico; the Governor General's Performing Arts Award (1993 ; Les Masques Awards (1998)-including Best Production for Young Audiences, Best Set Design and Best Sound Environment.

1989 **Terre promise/Terra Promessa (Promised Land)**
Scenario by Nino D'Introna, Daniel Meilleur, Graziano Melano, Giacomo Ravicchio and Monique Rioux. A co-production with Teatro dell'Angolo, Turin, Italy.
*Winner of the prize for Best Production for Young Audiences and Best Sound Production from the Quebec Theatre Critics Association, 1989. Winner of Best Sound and Visual Design, Theatre Festival of the Americas, 1989. Winner of the prize Premio ETI / Stregagatto, Rome (1991).

1986 **Parasols**
By Louis-Dominique Lavigne and Daniel Meilleur. Published by VLB Éditeur (1988). Translated into English by Linda Gaboriau as *Parasols.*

1987 **Clairière**
By Colette Tougas and Pierre Tousignant.
Translated into English by Linda Gaboriau as *The Clearing.*

1983 **Ni ange ni bête**
By Marcel Sabourin.
Translated into English by John Van Burek as *Neither Angel Nor Beast.*

1982 **L'Umiak (le Bateau collectif),**
by François Camirand, Yves Lauvaux, Michel O. Noel and Monique Rioux.
Published by VLB Éditeur (1984). Translated into English by John Van Burek as *Umiak, The Collective Boat.*

1981 **Les Petipain**
By Reiner Lucker.

1980 **Pleurer pour rire**
By Marcel Sabourin.
Published by VLB Éditeur (1984). Translated into English by John Van Burek as *Crying to Laugh.*
Winner of the Chalmers Children's Play Award (1982) for Best Canadian Play for Children.

1979 **On n'est pas des enfants d'école**
By Gilles Gauthier.
Published by Éditions Québec/Amériques and Centre de diffusion, P.P.M.F. (1980). Translated into English by Jack Zipes as *So You Think You're the Teacher,* and into German by Ragna Jeckel and Heinz Schersling as *Wir sind nicht Kinder des Schule.*

1978 **L'Âge de Pierre**
By Jocelyne France, André Gosselin, Daniel Meilleur, Benoît Ranger, Monique Rioux, Michel Robidoux and Colette Tougas.

1977 **La Vie à trois étages**
By Yves Dagenais, Gilbert David, Odette Gagno Louis-Dominique Lavigne, Jeanne LeRoux, Daniel Meilleur, France Mercille and Monique Rioux
Published by VLB Éditeur (1980).

1976 **Pourquoi tu dis ça?**
By Claire LeRoux, Marie-FrancineHébert, Michel Garneau and Claude Roussin.

À quoi qu'on joue?
By Monique Rioux, workshop directed by the co-directors.

1975 **Cé tellement "cute" des enfants**
B y Marie-Francine Hébert.
Published by Éditions Québec/Amérique (1980).

1974 **ne ligne blanche au jambon**
By Marie-Francine Hébert. Published by Éditions Leméac (1974).

C't'assez plate
By Marie-Francine Hébert.

Tu viendras pas patiner dans ma cour
by Marie-Francine Hébert.

1973 **Le Tour du chapeau**
by Marie-Francine Hébert.

YVES DAGENAIS–OMER VEILLEUX

"I give the audience the opportunity to invent their own words in the same way that I do it. A bit like Chaplin, I talk, but there's no sound, as if there were a window between the audience and me. But I never stop talking, commenting… So, inevitably, the audience invents their own text because I'm talking. If I open my mouth, there must be a text, logic. So they invent their own text. And often I think that with my shows people don't laugh at what I do but at the text they have invented for themselves and find funny. They find themselves funny because of the situation that I create."

– YVES DAGENAIS

Yves Dagenais, Delinquent-at-Large: Jester, Clown, Fool, Buffoon, Guillare

The traditions and roots of a character such as Yves Dagenais's Omer Veilleux go back to the Middle Ages, when a travelling clown always worked alone. In Dario Fo's handbook on clowning, called *The Tricks of the Trade* he describes what is called the *guillare*: "The *guillare* was the street performer of his day; he was the people's entertainer, but also the people's spokesperson, giving voice to satirical resentments felt by ordinary people against authority."

La cigarette tue, 1996. Omer Veillieux, a.k.a. Yves Dagenais.

Dagenais's clown character Omer Veilleux was a *guillare*, a street minstrel, a charming, delinquent fool who saw around him a world that was on the verge of collective insanity, stupidity and social alienation. Omer was "born" while Dagenais was working with an agit-prop company called Théâtre Parminou—as Yves describes it, Omer was a creation of necessity, a kind of accidental clown that developed in the hurly-burly of highly political street theatre. Omer was a clown whose mission was to spill the beans, to crack the jar, tip over the collective box of our own stupidities. Behind all the carefully timed and absurd humour was a serious artist with something to say about society, militarism, consumerism...the list is vast and rich for a character such as Omer Veilleux.

Omer Veilleux was born in the streets of Montreal, but very soon was on his way to festivals and theatres around the planet. During a tour to Colombia, the audience went wild. They filled the theatre, then stormed the theatre, and the military was brought in to restore order. I'm sure this is a remarkable event to happen to any performer. In our interview, Dagenais maintains that to this day that he is not sure why the Colombian public embraced his clown. Perhaps it was the delinquent—saying (or not really saying) the very thing that was on the collective mind of the public.

Also noteworthy is the fact that Dagenais created a clown for adults, not for children. This is a supremely difficult concept for North American audiences, who are more comfortable with the idea that clowns entertain at children's birthday parties or shill for furniture, flowers and hamburgers. North Americans consider clowns more a public nuisance than something to be entertained by.

It is a solitary act of determination, energy and skill to find the magic that a clown character contains, and then spill it into the theatre, ring or street. Omer Veilleux certainly made the world his playground, performing on four continents—taking the age-old *guillare*, bringing laughter, and more laughter by rocking the collective boat. Omer was, by all accounts, a delinquent-at-large.

I meet Yves Dagenais at the National Circus School in Montreal. I wait in the lounge as the students collect for classes in juggling, unicycling, tumbling and tightrope walking. The physicality of the international group is astounding, and the huge space—the school is housed in an old train station next to the Old Port in Montreal—is mind-boggling. It is hard to imagine a circus school in North America that does not have anything to do with animals or old circus families, but this has none of the tired traditions. There is a lightness and a playfulness here which I'm sure is due to the fact that most students are at ease walking on either their feet or their hands.

Dagenais has "hung up the nose" on Omer, mostly because of his extensive touring commitments with Les Deux Mondes, as well as teaching commitments at three different training institutions. He is also directing theatre productions in Montreal, and is perhaps the only circus and theatre crossover artist working in Montreal.

We find a quiet space, which I thought would be impossible at a circus school, and our conversation ranges from his early inspiration, to what, in fact, laughter is. Dagenais is full of stories of Omer's exploits, and he is a great interview.

▪ ▪ ▪

RA: Yves, as a career path, not too many people think about becoming a professional clown. How did you get inspired to start?

YD: I was exposed to the techniques of artistic entertainment very early because my father, without knowing it, would make us laugh at dinner time by doing all sorts of gags…he tried to make all four of us kids laugh by doing all kinds of gestures like double takes, triple takes. He had very precise gestures and expressions. And he loved Chaplin, Buster Keaton, all the early comics…

RA: So, your father was a big influence. With his natural abilities, did he ever want to work professionally?

YD: It was not possible. My dad was a natural comic; he often clowned around, but not on stage, just in everyday life. He was a travelling salesman. He sold all sorts of products. So through his work he had a very lively contact with people. But his clowning around was mostly for us. I don't think he did these double takes and techniques outside of our home. But at home he liked to play a lot. He loved Jackie Gleason. He loved American burlesque—Red Skelton and others. He knew them well and he watched them a lot. Sunday nights we were sure to be woken up for the Ed Sullivan show. We were young then. We waited for it. We went to bed before the Ed Sullivan show but we didn't fall asleep because we were sure that our dad would wake us up. When there were clowns or comedians, he'd come and get us. "Come see this, come see this," he'd say. So, very young I was exposed to this world of comedy. But I never imagined that it would become my trade, my profession, and my art form. However, I learned the effectiveness of gags, which is a technique in itself. Even if the same gag was repeated four times in a week, we laughed every time because it had some truth, some synchronicity, some sense of timing. Subconsciously, I understood this, I got it. I never really played with this technique. But later, in high school, I discovered theatre. There was a theatre course. It was a compulsory course, which I wouldn't have taken otherwise, because I didn't like theatre. I'm not sure I had even seen a play by then, maybe one, but not with school anyway. I was mainly anti-authority, anti-establishment; I was on the student council. It was in 1968-69-70. There were the May 1968 student protests, etc.

RA: Quebec was going through political upheaval; did you feel strong alliances to the political movement, rather than the ideas of what theatre could do for you?

YD: I was much closer to political matters than artistic ones. But then I got into theatre. I did my first play; I got my first job with Claude Poissant, in a collective creation. My first teacher was Jean-Pierre Chartrand, the actor. It wasn't when we did that first play that the revelation came to me, though. But it was an experience where I was able to put to use what my dad had taught me without knowing it. It was a satirical comedy about the Quebec situation. And the character I played required a lot of movement. So I had a lot of fun, but

I still didn't see it as doing theatre. In the meantime, the play was selected by the Canadian Association of Amateur Theatre, which was the precursor of the AQJT, (Association québécoise du jeune théâtre). We're talking about 1972-73. So I went to the ACTA festival in Quebec. It was a huge trip in a school bus. There were thirty or so people in the company. That's where I discovered a world that I didn't know: the world of collective creation and also contemporary theatre, like Ionesco. For a whole week I read tons of plays by completely crazy people.

At that time I also met a very, very young guy called Michel Tremblay.[12] There was also André Brassard.[13] All these young unknowns who were just starting out. And there was a sense of Quebec theatre. There were clowns like Chatouille and Chocolat all in a huge melting pot in Quebec City, in the same festival. But still I didn't imagine myself doing theatre. So I stopped and began working in a big print shop because I didn't know what to do after high school. Then one of my friends who had been in the play with me told me that he was planning on going to theatre school and was preparing his audition and asked me to play opposite him, to help him with his audition. I asked him: what is National Theatre School? Then I looked at the brochure and thought, "I'll apply too." So we agreed that we'd help each other for each other's auditions. And in the end I was accepted and he wasn't.

RA: I'm assuming the training at the National Theatre School was classical, and you had already got your feet wet in collective creation. So what was it like for you at the school?

YD: It was a shock for me when I was accepted because I didn't like theatre, classical theatre. It bored me to death. And I knew that was what they did at the school; I'd read all the information. I didn't see myself doing it for three years. But I'd have to. I'd have to wear a leotard even if I was a guy. And then that's where I fell in love with theatre, in theatre school. I discovered all these possibilities and openings, and all these books I'd never read before, that I didn't even know existed. First it was books about theatre, and that led to philosophy because theatre is inevitably inspired by philosophy or strives to be philosophy. A whole world opened up to me. And in my class there were people older than me who knew a lot, who read a lot. They were intellectuals who read Sartre, Nietzsche and Brecht... So I listened and went to the library a lot. When I discovered new names, I'd go read about them. Meyerhold, for example. That's how I learned: by reading what I heard about from my colleagues and in the classes. And quickly, even in the theatre history course, I could argue with the teacher about certain things because I read a lot about history.

RA: So it was at the NTS that you were opened up to all the possibilities.

YD: I began to be extremely interested in theatre. It was a whole world of theatre—and of art, because lighting and colour are intricately linked with theatre. I was interested in past trends and movements and in future ones. I'm a bit of a jack-of-all-trades. But there are limits and disadvantages to being a jack-of-all-trades, such as never going deep enough. I like Shakespeare, I like Molière, I like contemporary theatre, and I like collective production... It was the era of collective productions. I knew about collective production before theatre school, but not about the history of theatre. I'd already been part of at least two ACTA-AQJT festivals before theatre school. Even when I worked at the print shop I took a week off to go the festival. I said I was sick. I went because of the melting pot it was.

RA: Where did you begin to form the idea of your character, Omer Veilleux?

YD: At some point at the theatre school we did clown with Robert Dion.[14] Actually, he had been hired to teach us mime. We asked him to do some clown with us. We knew he was working on clown techniques at UQAM or somewhere with a group, and we wanted to try out some clown techniques. That was my first real initiation to the art of clowning.

RA: When you found out about clown, did you want to find more training?

YD: I left the school after two years, instead of the required three. I left because I wanted to change crowds. It was perhaps premature because to wait one more year before

12 Michel Tremblay, playwright and novelist.
13 André Brassard, theatre director and the former director of the National Theatre School, French section.
14 Robert Dion, artistic director of Dynamo Theatre in Montreal.

working with different people wouldn't have changed much. But I was all of twenty years old and I wanted to change the world by doing political theatre. And I did political theatre. First we founded a company called La Grosse Valise. It was my idea, as well as the cooperative model: everyone was equal, the director, the actors; everyone did everything. Most of the people came from the theatre section of the Ste-Thérèse CEGEP. The technical people acted and we did all the technical stuff. Some of our experiences were successful, others less so. There were eighteen or twenty of us in the beginning…but that quickly changed when we had to make a living out of it.

RA: That is a large team. How did you manage such a huge group?

YD: When I co-founded La Grosse Valise in 1975 I had just quit theatre school and didn't have a cent. So I had to make some money quickly. So, instead of political theatre, I first decided to develop a small clown piece, doing some juggling and using some techniques I learned at theatre school and perform it in the streets. The next day I went out into the street made up as a clown with a huge suitcase and a few ideas and performed a short piece. For a fifteen-minute piece I made twenty-five dollars. It was 1975. In those days my rent cost about sixty dollars a month. When I had worked at the print shop I made seventy-two dollars a week for forty hours. So I felt very rich with my twenty-five dollars. So I continued to perform on the streets several times a week, just on the side, because at La Grosse Valise we produced all sorts of other shows.

In 1978 I left La Grosse Valise to join Théâtre Parminou for two years. There we developed a clown show called *Ô Travail*. It was a show about exploitation, a Marxist class analysis on the exploitation of workers. It was commissioned by the CSN (Confédération des syndicats nationaux, Quebec's largest labour union).

RA: Were you still searching for your character at this point?

YD: That's where my clown name first appears. Because at the Parminou, the show was full of word games, puns, many

Les cols bleus, 1986. Omer Veilleux, a.k.a. Yves Dagenais. (Photo: Michel Dubreuil)

word associations that were very clownesque, not always very subtle. That's where "Omer Veilleux" appears, the name. With the show we toured all over Quebec. That's how the CSN became interested in us, and we began getting commission offers. So we started doing commissioned theatre. There was a lot of political unrest at the time, and we would start an intervention and the police would just charge into the crowd. So we'd have to get our stuff and take off. It was in those outdoor interventions that we learned to be light, set- and prop-wise…

RA: It sounds more like guerilla theatre, or agit-prop theatre.

YD: Basically, it was agit-prop theatre. We would go to encourage people to continue striking. We would come with arguments for continuing. At first we had sets and props but we soon learned that if the police came we should have as little stuff as possible so we would be able to take off quickly and not lose our things. So we learned a lot and developed a theatre that was efficient and clear: three minutes and we were off.

RA: It sounds like it was a pretty radical group, taking on the cops, the "system," and working with the extreme left. Did that affect your ideas on what social action theatre was all about,

L'affiche, 1983. Omer Veillieux, a.k.a. Yves Dagenais. (Photo: Michel Dubreuil)

and I'm speaking more about the Augusto Boal[15] model, social change through theatre?

YD: I was getting more and more into Marxist-Leninist ideas and into the Canadian Marxist-Leninist movement that was developing, so I left the Parminou theatre. For a time I went from company to company for different theatre projects. I also joined a movement where we tried to do agitation-type theatre. Then I was doing stuff more like distributing newspapers at factories at seven in the morning. I've done that too… I followed the movement until the eighties. Then I started thinking about all these ideas, whether they were actually real solutions to our problems. At the same time the feminist movement appeared, which radically questioned the values of all the political movements of the period because it showed how in the end all that activism didn't change the relationship between women and men much. In militant couples, it was still the woman who would be stuck cooking, taking care of the kids in the evenings. Nothing was actually changing. So that's how everything exploded, but for the better, I think. It might have brought something new, but that hasn't happened yet as far as I can tell. I think it's latent though, like still water. Nonetheless it has led to interesting soul searching.

RA: Probing the still water is the sign of an artist at work. For someone who had been a militant and a radical clown performer, basically an agitator, that must have been a big swing in attitude.

YD: It made me wonder who I was as an artist. I wondered how you could be militant and an artist at the same time. Because there is no freedom in ideology, while the artist must eternally, constantly contest. If you're part of a movement, if you're militant, you can't criticize… The artist's job is to reveal such things. It is important to be not neutral, but objective. She/he should have some distance from any organization or movement to be able to raise questions about every movement, left or right, about society in general. If your ideas are too determined, you are closed to any possibility of progress.

RA: What about changing the world?

YD: There were people who began saying, "Wait a minute, you're not changing anything, you're just siding with a system that privileges certain people even more than before." We heard about Russia, China, Poland, Albania, and realized that communism and socialism were really not that great. In the eighties everyone was questioning all that. I decided to get some distance from all of it and decided that I needed to be silent to think. I was still interested in clown work though. So I applied for a grant to the Canada Council, which I got. And, for a year, I worked on developing a character and writing a show that I presented in Montreal in an inexpensive theatre because I was quite broke. It was all about experimentation. And I wanted to remain silent; I didn't want to talk anymore. So I decided that Omer Veilleux would be silent. I felt that I'd already talked too much.

RA: The creation of clown theatre was a pretty radical idea. Were you looking for something to say as an artist/militant/clown?

YD: My first pieces were still very political, but not militant. I could criticize the left as much as the right. I did that in several pieces. I criticized unions. I felt much freer. But Omer Veilleux was meant to end after a year when my grant would run out. I was also working on other projects at the same time.

RA: Clowns are often perceived as children's entertainment. Was that a tough perception to change?

YD: Omer Veilleux was not a show for children. After my presentation in Montreal I got all these invitations. I was asked to perform at the Canadian Embassy in Paris, at the Cultural Centre. Then other people who had come to the show invited me as well. I toured Quebec and I went to Banff. It started very slowly, a tour, a festival. I did a summer theatre season with Omer Veilleux. I participated in the Montreal Mime Festival where still other people saw me. And in 1985 I participated in the first-ever Festival des Amériques that was attended by many producers and directors of other festivals because it was the first edition. After my premiere

15 Augusto Boal, theatre activist and writer; author of *Theatre of the Oppressed.*

there were many people of different nationalities knocking at the door of my dressing room saying they wanted to talk to me. That's when I got several firm invitations to many festivals. I had never thought of such an outcome. I just did this show with no particular plans for it. So of course, I accepted all the invitations with enthusiasm. I had just wanted to have fun. Nothing was planned. I'm not a career type of person. I still don't have one, by the way. I never tried to make a career.

RA: You created an accidental clown?

YD: You could say that. I started my tour. I went to South America. I had never gone there before. I'd been invited but had to find funding from here to go. It was a small festival with little money. They had invited me but couldn't pay any fee. So I asked for money from the Canadian government, and didn't get any. Finally the festival was able to provide my airfare but I had to pay for my baggage, which was quite expensive, and I had a technician with me. For the technician it was a trip, a week in South America. He'd never gone either. And there, in Columbia, my show turned out to be a mega-success. When I got there I didn't speak Spanish. I didn't know anything. I got to Bogotá, the world's most dangerous city, and the army was everywhere. It was a world I really didn't know. The next day we took the plane to go to Medellín in the south. My show was such a success that, to this day, I still don't get it. I was continually pestered by journalists; everyone wanted to be with me. I was asked to do three supplementary performances at the festival at 11:00 pm. And when I got to the theatre around 5:00 pm there were four or five hundred people outside waiting in line who didn't have tickets. So on the last evening the army came because of me. I still don't get it. My character somehow evoked for them delinquency and freedom. It was a freedom that they didn't have at the time. There was huge social pressure and a strong military presence there then. My show denounced the military; my character was delinquent with them... During my show, the army was circulating in the theatre with machine guns. And I wondered how they would take my last piece, which was anti-military. What would they do? I still can't get over it.

RA. That is a remarkable story. How did being in the spotlight, achieving that kind of success affect your ideas as a clown and artist?

YD: Often in other places people relate much more to what you do. Like in Finland. Or Bulgaria during the communist regime; that's when I understood why I stopped being militant. It was the last days of the communist regime. The day that I was coming back, Hungary had decided to join the Common Market. And from that came the toppling of the Berlin Wall and all the rest of the changes several months later. So when I was in Bulgaria it was really the last days of communism. And my show had the same success. I did supplementary performances at that festival too, because of the freedom and delinquency in my show. In Finland, for example, everyone, all the organizers, told me not to expect public reaction like in my own country because in Finland people don't react during the show; they talk about it when they get home. But the theatre went completely nuts; it was a huge party.

RA: Why do you think that is? Have you ever analyzed the response?

YD: I give the audience the opportunity to invent their own words in the same way that I do it. A bit like Chaplin, I talk, but there's no sound, as if there were a window between the audience and me. But I never stop talking, commenting... So inevitably, the audience invents their own text because I'm talking. If I open my mouth, there must be a text, logic. So they invent their own text. And often I think that with my shows people don't laugh at what I do but at the text they have invented for themselves and find funny. They find themselves funny because of the situation that I create.

RA: You are very complicit with the public; how do you gauge that from country to country or even place to place?

YD: When I started Omer Veilleux, I had several years of theatre experience behind me; I knew what kind of audience reaction I was looking for. It depends on the theatre and the country, of course, but basically it's always the same reaction.

For each gag I get the same reaction. I get the same reaction for the understanding of each piece. The audience understands the same thing everywhere in the world. And I think that I also control whether the audience will agree with a piece. So when I want the public to disagree, I plan it. Sometimes, of course, I get surprises.

RA: Have you ever totally misjudged the mood or temperament of your audience?

YD: I did a piece on abortion with two characters—Mother Teresa and the Pope—both of which I played. I knew that that piece would raise controversial questions. I also did a piece on child sexual abuse, which I knew would provoke a reaction, but I hadn't expected it to be such a strong reaction. People stopped laughing for the next three pieces. I didn't want the audience to laugh at the end of the piece, which was a punch, it was a kind of twist; while people laughed I turned everything around and suddenly everything became apparent, the sexual aggression which didn't show before. After that I wanted to take the public somewhere else, like in life, to say don't forget that this exists, but let's continue with other things. I wanted to make them laugh again afterwards. But it took at least two more pieces to get them laughing again. Sometimes it was hard. What I wanted was to slap them in the face, to say, "We laugh, but it's not really funny." I also did a piece on the École Polytechnique massacre. I eliminated it because it was really too much; it was only six weeks after the massacre. I didn't want people to forget, but for the public it was too much emotionally. Laughter is directed at insensibility/insensitivity, at the intellect, and not at sensibility/sensitivity. And people did not laugh because it was too touchy and too emotional.

RA: What makes us laugh?

YD: What makes us laugh? I teach a theoretic course on laughter. We spend the whole semester on laughter. Where does it come from? What makes us laugh? We even examine the physiology, the muscular system. We've discovered that the range of activity is very vast but also very restricted. It's restricted because it all comes from a single thing, from what's human. But because humanity is vast, the range opens up again like a funnel.

RA: Can you give me an example?

YD: Human stupidity, for one. It's still around and there's lots of it and it will always be around. As long as there is human stupidity I won't lack inspiration for my clown work. I

Le renard et la cigogne, 1986. Omer Veillieux, a.k.a. Yves Dagenais. (Photo: Michel Dubreuil)

personally find inspiration in stupidity, in everything that is contrary to reason. It is nothing too analytical or complex, just reason. That really sums it up. What does reason dictate? How do leaders, people, go against reason? For example, I think war doesn't achieve anything. Reason tells me to eliminate war. So I do a piece against war. Reason tells me not to join the army, because I can get killed or because I have better things to do. I'm more intelligent. That means that soldiers are not demanding. I really think so. Because it's crazy to do what they do; it's not intelligent. So I will ridicule soldiers in their intelligence and in their pride. I will humiliate them. That's how I function for several pieces. Sexual abuse is terrible but it's often due to too much trust and to its betrayal. So to address this problem of abuse of trust, I'll say beware of hockey coaches, beware of teachers, beware… Reason dictates this to me. It's not a Marxist analysis at all.

RA: In your work at the National Circus School, are you responsible for the training or formation of clown characters?

YD: I don't train clowns for the circus here. Actually, we don't train clowns here. We could never say that we train people to be clowns here because that takes a long time. It's a very long process for a character to find her/his maturity, her/his universe, her/his humour. So we provide them with the tools and techniques to continue developing their own personal clown world.

RA: You have an extremely varied career, teaching at several major institutions.

YD: I also teach at UQAM. There was a time when I'd be at the National Circus School in the morning, the National Theatre School in the afternoon and at UQAM in the evening.

La dernière facture, 1993. Omer Veillieux, a.k.a. Yves Dagenais. (Photo: Michel Dubreuil)

RA: What is the difference between circus students and theatre students at the National Theatre School?

YD: At the theatre school, it's a workshop. It's not a very long programme. It can be forty-five hours, at a rate of six hours a week or even less. It enables them to see their faults. Though I didn't do it to initiate them to the art of clowning, I discovered that what I told them about truth and acting depth was the same as their psychological drama teacher told them, exactly the same thing. Because their acting must be increased by ten for clown theatre. So I see their mistakes, their faults, as ten times bigger. As their acting begins to grow, they see what I mean by lack of depth or truth, by cliché, by unfelt, by inhabiting their character. It's hard to be naked in front of everybody. But once you've learned that "nudity" you can go back and do drama.

RA: You have worked extensively with Les Deux Mondes, particularly the character of young Maurice, in *The Tale of Teeka*. How do you find shifting between the clown complicity and mind set, to an actor in a play?

YD: With *l'Histoire de l'oie* it was the same approach. The only difference between clowning and drama is form. The work is about using imagination, about likelihood, about telling a story, about plausibility. I'm against psychology, even in dramatic theatre. That's actually what I teach more these days—a non-psychological approach to the character in theatre—much more than clown techniques.

RA: How would you define Omer Veilleux and what is your relationship with your clown character now?

YD: "Mister Omer Veilleux" has performed as much on clown stages as on theatre stages and mime stages. He's a bit of all of those and also none of them. I can't define him clearly and I don't want to. Was it said in Shakespeare's time that he was an excellent classic? When he was alive? No. When he was alive the critics didn't say that he wrote great classical plays. When I die they'll put me in some category. But now I'm alive and I can change all I want and go wherever I please. I'm not interested in having to situate Omer. To situate Omer is like fixing him. I'll fix other plays, but Omer I don't want to. Maybe I have a problem with him, perhaps a psychological one. But I don't want to fix him; I don't want to define him. He's a character.

RA: Are you still performing Omer Veilleux?

YD: Since I've been here at the circus school, and because of my tours, I don't do much Omer anymore. I toured for ten years with Omer Veilleux. At some point I was performing in *l'Histoire de l'oie* at the Quebec festival. After the premiere I was replaced for the rest of the performances and took the plane to Singapore to perform Omer. From there I came back to Toronto to perform the premiere of *l'Histoire de l'oie* at the World Stage Festival in English.

RA: It is astonishing to hear about an actor, any actor, who has stayed with a performance for so long. How do you keep *l'Histoire de l'oie* fresh and alive?

YD: To play a show for as long and as few times in a year is very rare. We've only performed some forty to fifty times in ten to eleven years. That's only four to five shows a year. And that's what's so great. It enables us to breathe and grow in between. So when we come back to the character we discover it all over again… Why is this happening this way? Or a gesture by another when we change languages…we perform it in four languages, so when we change languages we rediscover the music, an attitude. It's a permanent process of small nuances that the audience will never notice. It's a rediscovery of the text, of the directing, of the characters, each time. It's really extraordinary. We've been working on the show for fifteen years. Such an approach enables you to go to the limits of a show, of a character, of a play. When you continually change performance spaces you rediscover the show each time.

RA: What has working abroad for such a long time given to you as an artist?

YD: I've directed three shows abroad. It's given me the opportunity to not only go show what I do elsewhere but also to go work with other people. I worked on a show in Mexico; it was *Don Quixote*, with Mexican actors. Unfortunately, we couldn't finish it, but we got quite far. One show was in Uruguay. There I put on *Lysistrata*. And currently I'm finishing work with a Swiss circus. It's a small family circus. We're rehearsing in Montreal now. They leave in two weeks. Then when I finish *Amphytrion* here I'll go to Switzerland for ten days. So I work with people from other countries, often for several months at a time. Sometimes it's total immersion, like in South America. It's extraordinary. I learn so much from such experiences.

RA: Yves, as a teacher and a director, what do you see as the major problems for students after graduation?

YD: I find it so sad when actors have to go work as waiters. I think that there are too many theatre-training institutions in Quebec. The market is too small. We have a population of only seven million. The market is too small for the six major theatre schools in Quebec. There are two professional conservatories, two CEGEPS, the National Theatre School, UQAM and Concordia.

RA: Do you see a solution to this overload of creating too many actors?

YD: In all these theatre schools, theatre sections, departments, what are we training people for? Acting? Film acting? TV acting? What? It's a bit of everything of course, and we must address and combine the genres...we can't be too narrow. However, the different schools could specialize in different things, like film acting, for example... This would at least guarantee different outcomes for the different schools. These days that's what I've been thinking about.

RA: Do you see any young artists forming groups that emerge from some of these training institutions?

YD: It's harder now for students who graduate from theatre schools. When we were starting out there were local initiative projects (LIP). There were employment programs. Now there's no more money for things like that. There are some youth programs, but nothing that you can really do much with. However, when there were all those programs, there were many theatre companies that were not professional. They were amateurs. They didn't have any training. They didn't want to tour. The Parminou group was an exception. So that wasn't great either. People would go to theatre productions and they'd think that that was all theatre was about and not want to go anymore. And they were right. There'll always be the two sides of the argument. Is it better to blindly support young theatre? Or should we support young artists according to certain considerations?

RA: What do you think the attitudes of the next generation are?

YD: Today there are more and more young people who don't want to have anything to do with the institutions and who want to create their own companies. That's interesting.

RA: How is teaching at the National Circus School different from the National Theatre School?

RA: Circus is very different from theatre. In circus it is about developing an eight-minute number. You learn it intensively. That is what you do. In theatre you don't learn to do a single eight-minute scene by Shakespeare and perform it as a career. The principal activities in the circus are dance, trapeze, etc., which will be done over and over for ten years. The number can be improved with some small changes, and with costumes, sets and music. So it will be improved but it will be the same movements. It's very different—clowns are something else altogether. They don't come up with new pieces all the time; rather, they have their own baggage. They have pieces too, of course, but those are based on their personal baggage. It's a question of energy, of personal energy. Everything is based on personal energy, on humour, on one's particular type of personal humour.

RA: The space is also completely different; perhaps you could speak about that?

YD: The circus stage is a ring or 360°; it's very different from the classical proscenium arch or the Italian stage. But we do both here, at the National Circus School. We often develop work in Italian stage model because we have a small room where I'm alone with the students. But then we take it to the ring and we really have to adapt. When we present students' work-in-progress here it's also done in Italian stage mode. If we want to do it in a circle, we place the audience around the performance.

RA: Have you ever thought about what these two quite diverse groups could learn from each other?

YD: I've brought circus school students into the theatre school to work on projects together. There are also other initiatives and collaborations between the different theatre schools taking shape. The students from the Conservatory come here once a week to be introduced to the different disciplines of the circus: trampoline, acrobatics...to develop acting work in space. I think it's a great idea. So collaboration between the professional theatre training schools is on the way, but it's taking time. And what's becoming evident is that it's interesting, worthwhile, for all of them.

■ ■ ■

La Plage, 1987. Omer Veillieux, a.k.a. Yves Dagenais. (Photo: Michel Dubreuil)

THEATRE SMITH-GILMOUR

"We believe that the actor's imagination is at the centre of the artistic process and the actors must risk failing in order to find a new freedom. We believe that the purpose of art is to make people more fragile, tender and tolerant. In our work we write with our bodies. We believe that artistic diversity is what makes a culture healthy. Beyond linguistic, cultural and age barriers, we believe in a theatre of image and action that can make us feel by speaking to the heart. We lead the group through the process. Our primary work in adapting literature to the stage revolves around the attempt to capture the essence of the story: through essential images and text, essential gestures of characters."

—THEATRE SMITH-GILMOUR

Theatre Smith-Gilmour

We were deeply touched by Chekhov's short stories. The simplicity and humanity of his writing gave us an opportunity to explore the essential; to listen, see, and feel with the heart; to search for a real connection between the audience and actors, between fiction and reality. This is why we continue to do this work and why we continue to explore Chekhov; there is still so much more to learn from him. —Programme notes for *Chekhov longs…In the Ravine*

I first met Michele Smith and Dean Gilmour in Paris during the late 1970s while they were attending L'École Jacques Lecoq. Michele is an actor and director born in Corsica, France, and Dean, her partner, is an actor, director and teacher, born in St. Thomas, Ontario. Together, both as husband and wife and as a creative team, Smith and Gilmour have been creating, writing and touring their plays since the early 1980s. Over the years, they've discovered and pursued their passion for adapting works of literature into clown-based and imagistic theatre. Their latest plays, based on Chekhov's prose, both short and long stories, have been huge successes. Their performance is grounded profoundly in Lecoq's pedagogy, and over the years they have developed an impressive body of work.

Chekhov's Shorts and *Longs* have brought Theatre Smith-Gilmour out from the margins of the Toronto alternative theatre scene into the spotlight. The plays have now been performed across Canada, in Hong Kong, and will be touring to the United States, Korea and Taiwan. They have also found success in their hometown of Toronto, playing for fifteen weeks to sell-out houses. Is it the timelessness of Chekhov, or the performances full of heart, humour, modesty, melancholy, or a combination of all of these?

I was able to catch a performance of Theatre Smith-Gilmour's *Chekhov's Shorts* in Montreal a couple of weeks before our interview. The audience, which was composed mostly of seniors, entered the theatre with a sense of hushed expectation. They had been warned: this was "theatre of the imagination" and the expectation was that it could be a very strange evening.

There is virtually no set—the stage is empty save for a collection of tawdry suitcases, which sit on the forestage of the theatre. They are like a suitcase version of

Chekhov's Shorts, 2000. L-R: Dean Gilmour, Michele Smith, Patricia Marceau, Liisa Repo-Martell. (Photo: David Leyes)

matroshkas, the Russian nesting dolls, each one fitting into a larger one. The stage erupts with movement as Dean Gilmour, Michele Smith, Monica Dottor and Patricia Marceau begin the performance with choreography to klezmer-style music. The cast members are wearing goatee masks, long black coats and heavy boots, like a group of pre-Soviet comrades. In the blink of an eye, they have taken us from the barren stage to inside the postal train which races across the steppes of Russia. This is indeed theatre of the imagination and more specifically, theatre of essence—light, precise, and delightful, an eyeful and earful of stories that weave and chase each other, then nestle into the previous story.

The suitcases become everything—to begin to describe all the images that the suitcases create would be to cheapen the experience. Suffice to say that without any other props, these suitcases transform into chairs, train seats, musical instruments, hiding places, coffins, Russian nesting dolls, even a circus.

The images are exceptional—a woman lying on a suitcase is shoved towards the centre of the space by an ever-increasing number of suitcases, the absurd yet beautiful action conjuring up an image of time, travel and fatigue. Two babushkas slide onto stage riding on a suitcase. Light snow falls and the narrator, played by Gilmour, walks slowly towards the babushkas; there is something absolutely timeless and universal about the scene. There is a delicate and seamless transition from story to image and back to story, the result, a beguiling, emotionally clear and beautiful piece of theatre.

Originally Smith-Gilmour worked exclusively as a duo, focusing on their own Lecoq-based clowning style. Since the 1990s they have been interested in creating a larger ensemble. This vision of nurturing and developing an ensemble has led them to invite other artists to work with them—they follow a careful and rigorous method which encourages the individual creator/actors to discover within themselves what is called the "hidden story." This hidden story allows the rich and detailed inner life of the character actor to come to the surface, freeing the actor to really play and commit to the ensemble. This work pushes the group to the limits of creation and performance, which is the essence of their work, a playful and multi-layered fusion of storytelling, action, imagistic theatre and clown.

In addition to their work as writers and directors, both Michele and Dean teach extensively. Dean has taught at numerous institutions across Canada giving master classes and Michele has directed plays in Toronto. Our interview takes place in their Toronto home.

▪ ▪ ▪

RA: Dean, where did you get interested in physical theatre?

DG: I attended the University of Windsor and studied with Diana Kelly. It was a pretty much Canadian hybrid training, some English and American traditions.

RA: Any early influences?

DG: Yes, I saw Harro Maskow and Adrian Pecknold in high school; they performed a silent mime piece about an aviator. They were working with the Canadian Mime Theatre in Niagara-on-the Lake, and I heard that they were connected to Lecoq. This was in the early 1970s.

RA: Mimi, what about your early influences?

MS: In the late 1960s I was very interested in alternative sources. I didn't want to follow the traditional *conservatoire*, which was conservative, so it was not an attraction to me. Where I lived in Corsica, there was very little theatre; in fact it was mostly terrible. Then I saw Madeleine Renaud, wife of Jean-Louis Barrault in *Oh! les Beaux Jours*, which was a classical performance. Her performance was wonderful and childlike; she had a very clown-like presence. I also saw *The Bald Soprano*, and plays by Beckett and Ionesco, which were curious and crazy texts.

RA: Did you want to study theatre immediately?

MS: No, I wanted to study literature at university in Aix-en-Provence. Literature was a very important source, and given the radical times in France, I did not want to be in the mainstream.

RA: Dean, how did you get interested in studying at L'École Jacques Lecoq?

DG: When I was in my third year at the University of Windsor I had a very good friend who went to study at the Canadian Mime School in Niagara-on-the-Lake and there was a man teaching Lecoq work there. This friend told me all about the Lecoq work that they were doing and at the same time a teacher of mine, Bathsheva Garnett, saw Lecoq do his lecture-demonstration called "Tout Bouge" at the Wisconsin Mime Festival in 1975 and she also talked to me about the school in Paris. Between the two sources I decided I had to go there.

RA: Why did you want to study there after the University of Windsor?

DG: I was not really satisfied with my training, and I wanted to pursue something else, or rather, something more.

RA: Was L'École Jacques Lecoq the answer for you?

DG: I was a bit of a jock at Windsor—I played hockey, basketball—and so I was very much at home at Lecoq's school. Lecoq himself was a Phys Ed teacher; he combined sports, theatre and movement. He was also an intellectual who really taught us how to be intuitive, how to trust our creative impulses through movement. It had a pretty profound effect on me. Certainly this kind of training did not exist in Canada at the time.

RA: Michele, did you have early influences?

MS: I saw Ariane Mnouchkine's[16] work. It was an illumination—it was like an explosion for me. Yes, I would say a defining moment, so different, a theatre that was alive. After I found out she studied with Lecoq, I wanted to go there.

DG: Lecoq was a great teacher. He was a springboard. He taught us how to be artists, to work intuitively. He really had a blueprint on how to create theatre.

RA: Michele, what about your experiences at Lecoq's school?

MS: It was a very complete education. I was able to put my desire for physical expression and imagination and my love of fairy tales and stories and performance all together at the school. He gave me the idea that it is a pleasure to move, a pleasure to play, even if I am going to play a scene about war. It became so obvious. He also gave us a strong understanding of the classic traits of theatre; Greek tragedy, *commedia dell'arte*, melodrama, and, of course, clowns.

RA: So, Dean, you both returned to Canada and started a company and a family.

DG: Yes, our first show, which was called *Just Married*, was at the World Stage Festival in 1980. We have created twenty-six shows and played in twelve countries, and we have two daughters. We have been busy.

RA: Is teaching a critical part of Theatre Smith-Gilmour, keeping up the work and the teaching of Jacques Lecoq, or does it fill in the gaps?

DG: In the beginning Mimi and I taught clown workshops; there was a period of about five or six years where the two of us taught clown workshops, and it was really just clown. What we were concerned with was having a direct connection between our teaching, and what we were creating at that time. There was something about the clown workshops that didn't make sense. I didn't think it made much sense to teach people clown, just clown. People seemed to only want the "surface." You know, just looking for easy solutions.

RA: You mean get their red nose and go home?

MS: Yes, take a class, become a "clown" and that's it. We knew that it does not work that way. Even now, people want it easy. They say, "Please make me into a clown."

16 Ariane Mnouchkine, French director and theatre creator, who studied at Jacques Lecoq's school.

DG: In our own work, we were taking a lot of time, and developing the piece over a period of time. There was not an easy solution or a quick way to make the work.

RA: Is that the same for *Chekhov's Shorts*?

DG: I would say that with our play, *Dante's Inferno* and then with *To Cry Is Not So*, our style and process has evolved. This is where we really did collaborative work. This is where we began adapting literature and started to find our way of working in-depth and discovering exactly what our process is. We discovered by trial and error, success and failure that we needed or perhaps wanted to go under the surface to a deeper level, both with our collaborators and in teaching. This discovery of our vocabulary and our precise working process really began to feed all of our work—both teaching and performing.

Chekhov longs...In the Ravine, 2001. L-R: Dean Gilmour, Michele Smith, Liisa Repo Martell, Ann-Marie Kerr, Colombe Demers. (Photo: David Leyes)

RA: Where were you teaching at the beginning of your career?

DG: I started at York University, teaching neutral mask.[17] The director of the programme at York, Edith Nuckley, really loved this work. She was touched by it and felt it was very important. Neutral mask is a fundamental grounding, and then clown and *commedia* grow out of that. Now I'm teaching more *jeu*. For example, I recently taught at the National Theatre School. I take students through the creative process that Mimi and I go through. The teaching inspires us. We take the creative discoveries we make through teaching, then link it to the creative process of creating and writing new plays. One aspect feeds the other and vice versa.

RA: Does it really feed the creation process?

DG: Yes. What has been interesting is that in our creation process as a company, we don't analyze or speak about *jeu*, or any exercises that we do in the rehearsal room. In rehearsal, everything we do is for the creation. The work in rehearsal is essentially how to intuitively tell the story; it is the story that drives us in our work. What I find, more and more, is that in teaching classes, I am analyzing the work. What I discovered was that in the creation work, I don't analyze. I had to listen to my intuition. It kind of makes sense. You can't be analyzing and creating at the same time. If you are analyzing, you are out of it. Lecoq would say, "You can't show the students what to do. They have to discover it for themselves." So we were discovering how to mobilize our intuitions.

RA: Through your teaching, are you hoping to find people who share your detailed and passionate way of working—to find potential collaborators?

DG and MS: Yes, of course.

RA: Have you found actors who come directly through your teaching?

DG: Yes, we found Monica Dottor, who is currently performing with us in *Chekhov's Shorts*. She studied with me, and she has been touring. It's a real mentorship, and I would say that what she learned in the workshops brought her just to the doorway of jumping into the creative process.

RA: Your work over the years has certainly focussed on a deep understanding about the theatre, on how to tell a story, on complicity with the public, and a search for what is behind the text, the "hidden story", as you put it, which you have developed over a long period of time. How do you create an atmosphere of creativity so someone from "outside" can step into this process and say, "Hey, I can do this too"?

MS: It is difficult. We have made mistakes in the past. You know, a lot of actors come to us and say, "We want to work with you, and we have to trust someone." They seem to really want to work with us, but in fact, they have no idea what they are getting into.

RA: You mean what is going to be asked of them?

MS: Yes…or what is not going to be asked, but what has to be there!

RA: What is not going to be asked of you as a creator, but what must be there?

DG: Exactly!

MS: We ask actors to come in every day, day after day, even if it's just a few hours, and not see the end of the thing for six months. They can't, because they were not trained in this way. That is what students should be learning in school, because they can't learn it in "the business," because in "the business," standard rehearsal period is three weeks, and you know that is something we should think about as a community. It's not possible to create like this! You can get great productions in four weeks, by casting fantastic actors, but it's not the same thing. You don't create a piece, you create numbers from great actors, but it's not a total experience.

RA: Then is part of the ongoing training to find collaborators a big part of the global picture for Theatre Smith-Gilmour?

DG: We are always on the lookout for candidates. What I have been teaching, for instance, just recently at the

17 The neutral mask is a basic mask, the fulcrum mask for all other masks. Its perfect balance conveys a sensation of absolute physical calm.

National Theatre School, what ended up being the crux of the work we were doing, was what we call the "hidden story." It is our personal story, our personal desires for theatre, what we love, what we hate, and this hidden story becomes the *mise en scène*. Mimi and I have been developing this hidden story over twenty-five years, and yet this hidden story can't be discussed or analyzed. The way this thing gets nurtured, this hidden story...you can't just find it. There is no map of how this is going to happen. It's what happens by working moment-to-moment, piece-by-piece. So the virtuosity is that each actor has to get up on the floor and find something that mobilizes their intuition or, rather, makes them excited to play. The complicity, I think, comes from the amount of time spent working and working on your feet, on the floor. The actor has to be implicated—to be "into it." It pushes each actor to his or her own personal limits of endurance and patience.

RA: Do you find actors unwilling to go to that other step or level because of personal fear of risk?

DG: It's absolutely true in rehearsal that we face the unknown, and that's what we're teaching as well. This is intrinsically connected to the work that we do. We've developed this vocabulary by facing the unknown, encouraging actors to face the unknown, and to take risks.

MS: Yes, it can happen with our work, but very often the actors come and say, "What do you want us to do?" Well, we can't answer this question immediately because it must happen during rehearsal, so our reply is: "What do you want to do? What do you want to do in theatre, in this play, in this character?"

DG: So if the actors' imagination and intuition are not mobilized or realized on their feet in the space, then it won't happen.

RA: With this deep work, do you go through a lot of performers who are able to commit to the "equation" or do you keep an ensemble?

DG: Well, we've gone through different phases; in the early days there was not one person who came back. Maybe they would do two shows, maximum, but in fact we were not really thinking in those "ensemble" terms.

MS: I wanted to have an ensemble that could work with us all the time, but for us it was very hard to maintain because of money. We couldn't employ people for a long time.

DG: In the beginning, the primary thing was to create our own work.

MS: It was just the two of us. We started by doing two clown shows.

DG: Yes, two clowns shows.

MS: Then we felt that working, the two of us, was incomplete, and we felt that it would be fantastic to have a group, to be at least three, four or even five actors. But financially, it was impossible to do that. So we would do our own shows, just the two of us. Then occasionally, we would take an existing script—a Molière or Goldoni—and rehearse for four weeks. But the two ways of working were so different. We realized that we could not put as much imagination into the script because we had less time. It was more complicated because we had more people. In some of those shows there were as many as ten actors. Certainly going from a small ensemble of just two actors to working with as many as ten actors creates totally different sets of restrictions. We felt it was difficult to put the imagination into those restrictions. However, we had some success working with larger ensembles, particularly *The Green Bird*.

DG: After the first ten years we found we always had some dissatisfaction with the bigger ensemble shows, mostly because we felt that we were always working under the gun. Then we would go away and just work, the two of us, or create a three-hander like *In the Wings of Eden*. The restrictions were lifted, and we could really sense the full completion of the play, and felt the investment of our imaginations into the entire project.

MS: The same goes for *To Cry Is Not So*, which was a two-hander.

DG: Then in 1995, it became apparent that to really complete our vision we had to nurture group work—and find out how a group could function. Another thing that really drove us over the years was adapting literature—*Chekhov's Shorts, The Decameron, To Cry Is Not So*. We even used the Bible as the source for In the Wings of Eden and Dante Alighieri for Dante's Inferno. Our vision and vocabulary of working began to take shape—we were inspired by adapting shorter literary works and by a strong desire to try to find out how we could go further as actors and creators by nurturing a group.

RA: Your creative process has been honed through successful collaborations, and discoveries, real discoveries, and the pedagogical process, which seems to a first-time reader quite complex. Can you articulate this two-headed approach?

DG: What we have discovered is that for both the creative process in the rehearsal room hall and pedagogical process in the classroom there is an intrinsic marriage between *jeu*[18] and the problems of *jeu*. For example, there are always questions in writing by improvisation or there can be problems with acting and writing. By answering all the questions and dealing with the problems one by one, we can begin to answer the dramaturgical questions, help the actor deal with acting problems, then look to find what is the essential. All this work is done—for instance, finding the essence of a character—by working up on your feet. It's what we call *jeu*, or an acting proposition, or an improvisation. For example, the actor may only have a hunch about a character, but we encourage the actor to initially trust that hunch and go with it. With hard work and by putting some trust in the hunch, it can lead to the discovery or essence of that character. Then the character can begin to write, improvise, and finally, really be free to play. When the group transcends this period, the writing problems begin to solve themselves. By this point the group is able to tackle writing problems, because we understand so much more about the characters and what they need and want. All this feeds back into the *jeu*. So in fact, it is not a two-headed approach—it is a marriage. This connection between the two is intrinsic to our work. It is a very liberating process for an actor, and is implicated in the entire process, and the actors' imagination is at the very centre of this creating and writing and performing. It has been difficult for us to find actors because conventional actor training tends to separate these two forces—writing and acting. In conventional actor training, it is all about interpretation, which has nothing to do with the writing or creation. Or it might be about workshopping new plays, which is essentially dealing with a writer and writing problems. With this marriage of the two forces, we are looking for skilled actors who are not afraid to invest their entire imagination, who can deal with the whole vision of the writing, and who can fathom the complete project—all of it. This is the investment we ask of actors and if they accept, it will certainly help feed their acting. But it can be a huge personal stake.

Flying, 1993. Dean Gilmour and Michele Smith.

MS: But you know, when we invite actors into the rehearsal hall, we don't state it. We don't say, "Now you all have to have

18 *Jeu* or *jouer* are key words defined by Jacques Lecoq.They can be translated by many different words in English: to play/play; to act/acting; to perform/performing are all appropriate in various cases, but the noun "play" can be confusing since it also designates a written drama. From translator's notes: *The Moving Body*, by Jacques Lecoq, translated by David Bradby.

100% personal stake." You can't teach someone to mobilize their imagination, and then ask them for something personal about his or her life. It happens slowly, after weeks or months of working together. But what we insist on is that they be present all the time. And not to push too much. You know, not to be brutes!

DG: We are not offering all the "surface trappings" of a professional theatre, but a place where the actor is respected and is at the centre of the entire project. When we are working in our rehearsal space, there is no glamour. We have a small stage, an ugly grey curtain, and when you are up there and you are adapting materials, the adaptation has not happened yet. No one is handed a scene or scenario; we are creating the form as we work on our feet. The actor has to fill it every day and be present every day. There are even days when I have to admit to myself, "What a schmuck I am, and how small I am in this ugly space."

MS: It can be pretty depressing.

DG: It is what I call the "teeny talent time moment." Then as an actor, there is this danger and this risk; there is only one thing you can say, which is, "I believe that this is what I want theatre to be." It's what is confronted every day in our rehearsal hall. There are no donuts, there are no administrators pushing paper at you with schedule changes. There is nothing that gives actors, directors and designers—everyone—the feeling of how important they are. In our rehearsal hall, each person has to find the importance deep inside of him or her and when that discovery is revealed or made, it is a huge resource for the group. This feeling of finding what is important from within rather than from without is what I call the real trappings of professional theatre. It was a huge discovery for me and it only comes from personal experience. A few years ago we were performing Sean Dixon's *Sam's Last Dance*[19] at the Theatre Centre on Queen Street in downtown Toronto. Previously it was an old legion hall and it was a dump, a dive. I was sitting in the basement after the show having a beer with one of the technicians and I said to him, "You know, if you started to clean this place today, in three weeks of non-stop work, you might make a small dent." That's how filthy the place was. I was sitting there and I had this revelation, "This is it, I've reached the pinnacle of my career." For a small independent theatre company in downtown Toronto, the Theatre Centre was the top. To go beyond that, in Toronto, you needed a stroke of luck. It was a profoundly depressing thought. I was so depressed and thought to myself, "This is terrible. What am I going to do?" Perhaps it was a purely mid-life crisis depression, but I realized that it wasn't the kind of space I was working in that mattered, it was the space inside of me and that I carried all Jacques Lecoq's work inside of me and the possibility for Mimi and me to create more work lived inside of us, and it was not the superficial trappings of a professional theatre, the size, number of seats, etc. I realized that this is a huge resource, not a deficit. We did not have to follow the conventional path, seeking endorsement and waiting for the magic phone call, or hoping for the brilliant review.

RA: More surface trappings of professional theatre?

DG: Exactly. Someone endorses you. All of this waiting in this stupid profession, waiting to be endorsed. You work for over twenty years and hope someone is going to come along and say, "Bravo, Dean and Mimi. You've put in your years, now we are going to elevate you and here is the big payoff." Well, I'll be frank—there is no big payoff.

MS: No one comes along and says to you, "You can now go to the penthouse."

RA: Your vision, or what you have to say, is coming from a pretty profound place. And it's deeply embedded in all of your work.

DG: This conviction I have that every story has a hidden story comes to me so fundamentally from my life. My parents were divorced when I was a kid, a baby. So as I grew up, I heard a story about what happened. And the rest of my life has been spent trying to find out what the real story was...the hidden story that no one told, that no one could tell, because of dignity, because of keeping face...so the story is in bits and pieces, and it slips through your fingers. You get a bit of the puzzle, and that's what creation is...there is a hidden story. No one can tell this hidden story. There is no map to it. You just search for it, little by little. You find a piece and it costs a

19 Smith-Gilmour collaborated with Theatre Columbus and the Toronto writer Sean Dixon to produce *Sam's Last Dance*.

lot to find that piece, and that piece leads you to another, and then, little by little, you start to form something.

DG: For me it was a really healthy and wonderful realization that came out being horribly depressed. I was depressed at all the negative prospects. But instead it became a part of a wonderful re-evaluation: "There is no big payoff. That is so much bullshit." So, my answer to myself was to accumulate the moments of my life as a professional artist to what I want it to be. Then I can take these moments into rehearsal and we can improvise, tell a story and create a play. You know, to tell a story can be such a fantastic experience. The desire to tell stories brings us to working on Chekhov. Now, as artists, we're living in the world of Chekhov.

RA: What so attracted you to Chekhov's writing that you dedicated a period of your life to illuminating his stories?

DG: I'm convinced that there is a special quality in Chekhov, the man. He was modest. His writing has modesty. This great genius had a modesty that we admired and wanted to convey. He was a medical doctor, and I'm wondering what medicinal powers Doctor Chekhov put into his stories to heal us all. Chekhov's stories have had a fantastic medicinal effect on us. We feel this when we travel around the world telling his stories.

RA: You've managed to build an audience in Toronto as well as take your work beyond the boundaries of downtown Toronto, and Canada. Has it been tough to reach an audience when you don't exactly have a home?

DG: We were part of the Poor Alex Theatre Group in the eighties. While we were there we managed to build a small following. Then the group collapsed and we lost our home audience. Now we have been playing at the Factory Theatre Studio Theatre for about five years. This new initiative has really helped.

RA: So the Factory Theatre has been a healthy choice for your company's visibility.

MS: Yes. It has really been Ken Gass.[20] It's part of his vision to nurture new work and he is doing a fantastic job. It's a two-way arrrangement: we bring a new play to the Factory Theatre, and the Factory gives us a place, an anchor. We can develop the work here in Toronto, then tour. Ken always came to see our shows even when we didn't have a success. He also supported us when we had trouble with the OAC (Ontario Arts Council). Layne Coleman, the artistic director of Theatre

To Cry Is Not So, 1989. Dean Gilmour and Michele Smith.

20 Ken Gass, artistic director of the Factory Theatre in Toronto.

No Escape, 1983. Michele Smith and Dean Gilmour.

Passe Muraille, was also was very supportive. He said to the jury that was asking us to work with writers, "They have to do what they are doing. They are good at working the way that they work. Don't try to change that." Now, many years after he defended our work, we have a real success with *Chekhov's Shorts*. Layne really helped us.

RA: What are your long-range touring plans?

DG: We went through a time when our kids were smaller when we toured less. For about six years we didn't tour at all. But touring has always been a goal. It's kind of like the artistic process—one thing leads to another, leads towards the next step. Now that *Chekhov's Shorts* has a life of its own, I think the bottom line is to keep creating new work, keep searching for like-minded collaborators, and tour when the opportunities present themselves.

RA: To wrap up, we've talked quite a bit about process—what is the experience you want to leave the audience with?

DG: The process is what has driven us to further understand, to mobilize our imaginations. We want to find stories that are rich, funny and alive, but more than anything we have the intense desire to make a connection, to have a connection between the actors and the audience, and to touch what is essential about being human.

MS: For me art is about pleasure. Not just pleasure for pleasure's sake, but there has to be pleasure in it.

DG: There was a Russian filmmaker who said: "Art should make people more tender, more generous, more tolerant." For Mimi and me, we feel that this statement captures "why" we do this work.

MS: Our work in *Chekhov's Shorts* reflects, I feel, the best part of what we want to say. It is profoundly tragic, comic, political and poignant. It's about the human desire to hear and listen to stories, to be touched and moved by an image or a metaphor, to make the invisible visible. And for a few moments, all of us in the theatre share those moments.

▪ ▪ ▪

EXCERPT FROM CHEKHOV LONGS...IN THE RAVINE

THEATRE SMITH-GILMOUR

Dean appears on the stage, thinking,. Crosses USC to the bricks.

NARRATOR: *(Picks up one brick.)* Russia 1899. *(Picks up another brick and clops the two bricks together like horses' hooves.)* Many characters. *(Puts the two bricks on the floor DS in a line.)* There's a landscape. *(Goes back to pick up two more bricks and places them in the line of bricks DS.)* And a crescent moon. *(Goes back to pick up two more bricks.)* Bou...bou... *(Goes back DS to place the bricks in the line DS.)* There is bird called a bittern, which cries somewhere far, far away, sounds like a cow shut up in a barn. *(Goes back to pick up two more bricks.)* There's a brickyard. *(He hums the song from the end of the play and places the two bricks in the line DS, builds church.)*

Ukleyevo.

The village of Ukleyevo lay in a ravine so that from the high road and the railway station you can just see the belfry of the church *(Stands, looks at church. Comes back down.)* and the three chimneys of the cotton factories. *(Building the chimneys, creating puffs of smoke, stands.)*

Ukleyevo.

(Goes and picks up three bricks, brings them DS and places them in a pile.) Whenever anyone asked what village it was they were told, "That's the village where the Deacon ate all the caviar at the funeral." When the skinny little Deacon saw the caviar he bolted for it and began eating greedily. Everyone said, "Stop eating the caviar, stop eating the caviar, there has to be enough for everyone," but the Deacon was petrified with pleasure and went on eating until it was all gone. *(Makes gross eating sounds.)* All four pounds of it.

The village was never free of fever and smelled of refuse and acetic acid from the manufacture of cotton. The cotton mills were owned by the Khrymin Seniors and the Khrymin Juniors, who were constantly quarrelling and taking each other to court. On holidays the Khrymin Juniors would drive through the streets of Ukleyevo running down calves with their droshkys. *(He crushes with the bricks and then begins building the tanyard with three bricks.)* The tannery made the water in the little river stink, polluting the fields and plaguing the peasants' cattle with anthrax. *(Cow sounds.)* The tannery was ordered closed *(Puts tannery bricks down.)* but went on working in secret. (*Rubs the bricks together.)* The district doctor and police chief were paid ten rubles a month to keep their mouths shut.

Starts dismantling the village bricks to create house.

In the entire village there was only one decent house made of brick. It was occupied by old Gregory Petrovich Tzybukin *(Lies down on his side and laughs.)*, a merchant from Yepifan, who kept a grocery store but it was just for appearances. *(Sits up.)* In reality he sold illegal vodka, lent money at interest and traded in anything that came to hand: cattle, hides, grain, pigs. When magpie feathers were wanted abroad for ladies' hats he made thirty kopecks on every bird. All in all, he was a resourceful old man. *(The house now becomes the counter.)*

TZYBUKIN: Staz, Yakov, Feodor, come on in. You want some tea? *(Wink, wink.)* That'll be forty kopecks. That's the price, boys. Take it or leave it. I knew you'd see it my way. *(Pours vodka, puts money in drawer.)*

NARRATOR: On Sundays, Old Grigory Petrovich, dressed up in his shiny top boots, would harness his black stallion to his racing droshky and drive through the streets. If the peasants came up to him with their petitions, he would bellow...

TZYBUKIN: Why are you standing there? Move on. God will provide!

NARRATOR: He hated the peasants, they disgusted him, but he loved his family more than anything on earth. He was a widower with two sons. His favourite son, Anisim, was a police detective in the big city.

Mimi backs out USR.

ANISIM: You know...I've got the eye. That's right. I've got the eye. I see a peasant at the market selling a shirt and I say, "Hey, that shirt is stolen." And it turns out...the shirt was stolen. How do I know? I just told you! I've got the eye. Anybody can steal a shirt but to keep it is another thing. The earth is wide but there's no room for stolen goods. *(She steps back in.)*

NARRATOR: Anisim was rarely home. Tzybukin's younger son, Stepan, had gone in for business but no great help was expected from him, as he was both lame and hard of hearing. *(Mimi walks out USR as Stepan looks out to the audience and starts meandering towards USL.)* He would walk about the streets staring absent-mindedly, now at the houses, now at the sky overhead. *(Stepan exits USL. Aksinya enters cobra-style DSL.)* Stepan's wife Aksinya was a handsome woman with a good figure. Tzybukin regretted that she hadn't married his elder son Anisim as Stepan had no appreciation for female beauty. *(Aksinya rolls CS behind Dean.)* No sooner had they married, than Aksinya began to demonstrate an extraordinary gift for business.

Aksinya kneels behind Tzybukin. Tzybukin and Aksinya conduct business in the shop.

AKSINYA: Stepan! Two more cases of vodka! *(Out to customer.)* Five rubles.

AKSINYA/TZYBUKIN: *(Together.)* Hey, hey, hey. That's the price, boys. Take it or leave it. Forty kopecks? What do you think I am, stupid? Get outta here! I don't need your business!

AKSINYA: *(Bartering.)* What are those? Chickens? I'll give you two cans of sardines for all those chickens. Three cans? Are you crazy? I knew you'd see it my way.

TZYBUKIN: *(At same time as Aksinya.)* Whatcha got there? Cattle hides? I'll give you two pounds of sugar for all those cattle hides. Three pounds of sugar? Are you crazy? I knew you'd see it my way.

They confer and tap their fingers waiting for customers.

TOGETHER: Hey, Jacov/Ivan (Staz/Feodor), hey, you want some tea? That'll be fifty kopecks. That's the price, boys. Take it or leave it! *(Laugh, pour tea, take money, confer.)*

AKSINYA: Oh Papa!

TZYBUKIN: What a daughter-in-law! What a beauty!

Aksinya kisses him and exits USR.

NARRATOR: Less than a year after his son's wedding old Tzybukin could not resist getting married himself. *(Varvara enters DSR, sees the windows and starts to silently mime cleaning them.)* No sooner had Varvara Nikolaevna moved in than everything in the house seemed to brighten as if new glass had been put in all the windows. *(She makes squeaking noises, crosses DSL and continues to mime with squeaky noises.)* Varvarushka! *(She pulls out a comb and starts combing Tzybukin's hair, speaking gibberish to Tzybukin. She squeaks on his head and teases his hair up.)* There was something new, something gay and light-hearted about Varvara Nikolaevna. *(Varvara flattens his hair.)* Beggars and pilgrims began to come into the yard, a thing which had never happened in the past.

VARVARA: *(Varvara goes to window DSR, sees the peasants, motions.)* Stay there. I'll be right down. *(She exits USR.)*

NARRATOR: Varvara would help the peasants with gifts of bread, old clothes and money.

STEPAN: *(Stepan enters USR.)* Papa! Papa! Mama Varvarushka just took five ounces of tea from the shop. Five ounces! *(Looks out window.)* And she's giving it to the peasants! Wh-wh-where do I write it down? Which column?

TZYBUKIN: Varvarushka!

Stepan goes USC then right looking for Varvara, sees her and crosses USC. Varvara enters USR and goes to Tzybukin.

TZYBUKIN: Varvarushka, if you want anything out of the shop, take it, my dear. Take it and be welcome; don't hesitate, little Mamma.

VARVARA: Thank you. God bless you. *(Exits USR.)*

STEPAN: *(Following Varvara off.)* Mama Varvarushka, if there is anything you want, help yourself.

NARRATOR: Tzybukin tolerated Varvara's generosity, but still, during local church holidays, while she was in her room polishing the icons and lighting the incense, he would sell the peasants bad vodka and tainted salt meat that smelled so bad you couldn't stand by the tub of it.

TZYBUKIN: *(Lifts bricks off the tub. Smells terrible, holds meat out.)* Here! Take it or leave it.

NARRATOR: In those oppressive, murky days when the factory workers lay rolling in the mud stupefied with bad vodka and sin hovered in the air thick like fog, Varvara's charity had the effect of a safety valve in a machine. At night, when people were going to bed, an expensive concertina was played in the Khrymin Junior's yard. If the moon was full, those sounds filled the heart *(Stands.)* and Ukleyevo no longer seemed a wretched hole.

■ ■ ■

PRODUCTION HISTORY OF
THEATRE SMITH-GILMOUR

2002 **Chekhov longs...In The Ravine**
By Gilmour and Smith with the company
In association with Factory Theatre
Winner of 4 Dora Mavor Moore Awards: Best Actor, Best Director, Best New Play, Best Production.

Chekhov's Shorts winner of Montreal Theatre Critics' Award for Best Ensemble

Chekhov's Shorts
Second remount at Vancouver Firehall Arts Centre

Chekhov longs...In the Ravine
By Gilmour and Smith with the company
Carrefour International Festival

Chekhov's Shorts and Chekhov longs...In the Ravine
Factory Theatre Mainspace
Co-Production in Rep

Ward 6 (Part III of Chekhov Cycle)
Workshop production

2001 **Chekhov's Shorts**
Third remount at Factory Theatre. Tour to Edmonton, Vancouver, Dartmouth, Montreal, Hong Kong.

Chekhov longs...In The Ravine
By Gilmour and Smith with the company
Workshop production

2000 **Chekhov's Shorts (remount)**
By Gilmour and Smith with the company
In association with Factory Theatre

1999 **Chekhov's Shorts workshop**
By Gilmour and Smith with the company
Helen Gardiner Phelan Playhouse

Chekhov's Shorts
By Gilmour and Smith with the company
Factory Theatre
Nominated for Chalmers Best Canadian Play Award
Winner of three Dora Mavor Moore Awards: Best Actor, Best Director, Best Production

1998 **The Cherry Orchard**
By Anton Chekhov
Canadian Stage Company, co-produced with Theatre Columbus

Dante's Inferno
By Gilmour and Smith with the company
Factory Theatre, in association with Factory Theatre

1997 **Sam's Last Dance**
By Sean Dixon
The Theatre Centre, Toronto

Only Canadian theatre company invited to Cultural Capitol of Europe celebrations In Thessaloniki: performed **In The Wings of Eden**

Dante's Inferno
Workshop presentation
By Gilmour and Smith with the company
Factory Studio Theatre, Toronto

1996 **Founding members of The Group of Seven Theatres**

Kaldewey, Farce
By Botho Strauss
Canadian Stage, Toronto

1995 **The Time and Place**
By Botho Strauss
Factory Theatre, Toronto
Four Dora Mavor Moore nominations

Strangers In The Night
By Herbert Olschok, Gilmour and Smith
Premieres at Begegnungen '95 International Theatre Festival Chemnitz, Jena, Factory Theatre, Toronto

Le Malade Imaginaire
By Molière (In French)
Canadian Stage, Toronto
Two Dora Mavor Moore nominations
Dora Mavor Moore Award

1994 **The Decameron**
By Gilmour, Smith and Rocca
du Maurier World Stage, Toronto

1993-98 **In The Wings of Eden**
By Diane Cave, Gilmour and Smith
The Poor Alex, Toronto, Chemnitz,The Tarragon, Toronto, Plauen, Dresden, Edmonton, Winnipeg, St. John's, Chisinau, Sibiu, Belgrade, Shopje, Thessaloniki, Calgary, Kingston, Ontario, Dartmouth, Nova Scotia

The Poor Alex Group forced out of The Poor Alex Theatre

1991 **The Serpent Woman**
By Carlo Gozzi
Adaptation by Jason Sherman, Gilmour and Smith
The Poor Alex, Toronto
Dora Mavor Moore nomination

1990-93 **To Cry Is Not So**
By Jason Sherman, Alex Stockwell, Gilmour and Smith
Inspired by Julio Cortazar
The Poor Alex, Toronto. Victoria, Edmonton, Vancouver, St. John's, London, Oxford, Brighton, Leicester, Beaumaris, Edinburgh, Amsterdam.
Four Dora Mavor Moore nominations

1990 **The Imaginary Invalid**
By Molière
The Poor Alex, Toronto

1989 **The Miser**
By Molière
The Poor Alex, Toronto

Bonnie And Clyde Are Dead
By Banuta Rubess
The Poor Alex, Toronto

1988 **The Dispute**
By Pierre de Marivaux. Translated by Smith.
The Poor Alex, Toronto

Trouble Is My Business
By Gilmour and Smith
The Poor Alex, Toronto
Dora Mavor Moore nomination

1987 **Co-founded The Poor Alex Group with Crow's Theatre and Theatre Columbus**

Rites of Spring
By Theatre Smith-Gilmour/ Theatre Beyond Words
The Poor Alex, Toronto
Dora Mavor Moore nomination

Carmen, The Sequel
By Gilmour and Smith
The Poor Alex, Toronto

The Green Bird
By Carlo Gozzi
Adaptation by Diego Matamoros, Gilmour and Smith
The Poor Alex, Toronto
Four Dora Mavor Moore nominations
Chalmer's Best Canadian Play nomination

1986 **You Either Fly Or Fall**
By Gilmour and Smith
The Poor Alex, Toronto

Commedia, A Tale Of Passion
By Carlo Gozzi.
Adaptation by Gilmour and Smith
Theatre Centre, Toronto

1985 **Carmen, Opera For Two Clowns**
By Gilmour and Smith
Theatre Centre, Toronto

1984 **O Canayen!**
By Gilmour and Smith
Theatre Passe Muraille, Toronto

1982-85 **No Escape**
By Gilmour and Smith
Toronto, Saarbruecken, Rome, Hamburg, Nuremberg, Bonn, Vancouver, St. John's, Newfoundland, Copenhagen, Avignon

1981 **Just Married**
By Gilmour and Smith
du Maurier World Stage, Toronto

1978 Dean Gilmour and Michele Smith graduate from L'École Jacques Lecoq, Paris.

THEATRE COLUMBUS

"We laugh at the same things, and we cry at the same things. I wonder if all people who do comedy have this well of sadness. We both have a huge well of sadness, and because of that, we have to do comedy. We were always interested in that exploration."

—LEAH CHERNIAK AND MARTHA ROSS

Theatre Columbus

On a nondescript kind of typical no-weather grey November morning in Toronto, I find myself walking through the hipper-than-thou neighbourhood around Queen Street West. I've arranged a meeting with Martha Ross and Leah Cherniak, who are the actor, director, writer, and clown team behind Theatre Columbus. Both Martha and Leah completed their training at L'École Jacques Lecoq in the early 1980s.

Since returning to Canada, in the mid-eighties, and now for over the past twenty years, they have created an eclectic body of work, from the early clown-based works like *My Dinner with Jerome*, *The Anger in Ernest and Ernestine* and *The Betrayal*, to the wonderful collaboration with novelist and playwright Ann-Marie MacDonald, *The Attic, the Pearls and Three Fine Girls*. Their work has captured the imaginations of audiences throughout Canada, and productions of their plays have been mounted in the United States and Cuba.

Their plays are laced with a subtle and subversive humour, which is deeply connected to their own emotional temperaments. Anger, melancholia, loneliness, and doubt have inspired and informed the writing and creation of original plays.

Until We Part, 1984. Leah Cherniak, Martha Ross. (Photo: Rolf Cutts)

What makes this duo so unique is that the process of creation is so completely open. The acting ensemble and creative core remains the same—Cherniak and Ross, who then invite other actors and creators join them on various projects, resulting in a very personal and intimate playing style. The emotional clarity and precision of its writing is also one of the hallmarks of the company. Their signature is a well-honed, ingeniously crafted physical theatre which combines traditional European clowning techniques with contemporary issues and witty dialogue. All of their work reflects their passion and drive to create original comedies, linked to the great traditions of *commedia dell'arte*, melodrama, burlesque, and clown.

Since the inception of the company in the early eighties, they have found an audience which follows their smartly constructed plays that push the comic and tragic edge. For example, in a hilarious scene from *The Anger in Ernest and Ernestine*, the lead couple, played by Martha Ross and Robert Morgan, wildly debates the merits of writing a letter of complaint. The scene begins with clown-like innocence and hilarity, but as the intensity of the content of the letter evolves, anger, even rage creeps in and overwhelms the two clown characters. This is the essential edge—both the comic and tragic are revealed, and as this outrageous behaviour escalates, the letter—the relationship—tears at the centre.

Our conversation takes place at one of the ubiquitous Starbucks cafés. The Starbucks quickly fills up with young, hip downtown Toronto mothers, who stop in for a café latte. The café is filled with the sounds of little babies calling and crying, which seems completely appropriate for the interview. Our conversation is more of a round, with ideas and laughter bouncing around the table. It is evident that Leah and Martha are close friends and have managed to keep a working relationship and a close personal relationship, even while running a small theatre company. I can feel that these two women have shared many laughs together and probably many creative differences, but their impish energy is a joy to witness.

■ ■ ■

RA: Leah, when did you get interested in theatre?

LC: I went to The Free School in Toronto. There was no theatre programme, but a drama teacher was brought in who taught us Method Acting. My next early memory is of the YMCA, and Jim Garrard,[21] who was a super hippie. Jim worked with a group on a show called *The Rape of Futz*, which was closed by the police. It was a pretty impressionable moment for a thirteen-year-old on the power of theatre.

RA: Martha, where did you get your early training?

MR: I grew up in Burnaby, BC, and ended up at Simon Fraser University. I first got into theatre with an ex-boyfriend of Robin Patterson; she was my English teacher, so I was pretty aware of Robin.

RA: Robin Patterson from Theatre Beyond Words?

MR: The very same!

RA: Leah, what early inspirations led you to a creative career?

LC: My beginnings were not literary, although I loved books, and was a precocious and early reader of Hermann Hesse and the French existentialist writers. I was much too young, although I did think it was cool to read these authors. I also was involved with dance and movement and was pretty active in the sports scene, in particular, track and field.

RA: And what about you, Martha? Were you always interested in movement and physical expression?

MR: I always loved dance and movement, and I got into the modern dance world at Simon Fraser. I felt I didn't quite belong. I didn't know what it was. I think I probably realized just how disciplined you had to be in order to become a professional dancer. Then I was wandering in one of those freak snowstorms on Burnaby Mountain and I saw this notice saying: "Auditions for a play for the Theatre Department." It was an audition for a wild musical written by two ex-Jesuit priests which was called *The Brothers Karamazov*. It had everything, with references to *Long Day's Journey into Night*, Frank Sinatra...it was a great post-modern romp with great music. I had the smallest role; I played Grushenka, who gets cut in half, then she becomes a raging feminist...and I played Grushenka's legs! Not even a whole role, half a role!

RA: Martha, was there a moment when you thought that this particular style was meant for you?

MR: You know, my relationship with theatre was all very serendipitous. I never decided that one day I was going to go on stage. I always had a leaning towards dance, which was my big thing, even after a "foray" with the SFU mime troupe. There was no text, and it was back in the days when mime was fashionable. It was a very exciting time at Simon Fraser University; it was very vibrant—all the anti-war protests. I have never been wealthier than then, because there were jobs on the campus that paid ten dollars an hour, and I paid fifty dollars a month for rent. I was able to luxuriate in ideas, and protest, and do all those great student things. I truly did love it. Then the director of the programme pulled me aside one day and said, "You can't do this Method Style acting. Perhaps you should think about, I don't know...Buddhist theatre." I couldn't do actions. Although he had a great deal of respect for physical theatre, he didn't know how to access it. In the end, he said to me that I should look for something else to do. So I left SFU and went to work in the fish plants and made a ton of money. My boyfriend moved to New York,

21 Jim Garrard, playwright, teacher, actor, director and filmmaker, was the founding artistic director of Toronto's Theatre Passe Muraille.

and basically said to me, "I want to find myself, to go away." I decided this was the perfect time to go to Toronto to visit some friends, explore by taking some theatre classes just to see what it was about...and if my boyfriend changed his mind, I wouldn't be that far away.

RA: Leah, you went to university for your post-secondary education?

LC: Yes. I went to the University of Toronto's drama programme at University College for four years. It was a good time, and I had two or three teachers that made an impression on me, but mostly it was reading: Brecht, Meyerhold, Peter Brook, Stanislavski, Artaud. Also, beginning to understand the physical life, which is at the centre of the work, and discovering that images are very important. In my last year, I directed *Orphée* by Cocteau.

RA: Leah, how did you end up attending L'École Jacques Lecoq?

LC: In 1980, I met Dean Gilmour. I was in a show, and he liked it very much. He suggested that I attend Lecoq, which I thought was a good idea, although I was considering a MA in acting and directing at Brandeis University in the States.

RA: What was your time like at the Lecoq School in Paris?

LC: I loved all the work! I loved living in Paris. I spent two years at the school, learning the forms and the styles. And of course, Lecoq's pedagogy was very influential. Two of the important teachers at the school, Monica Pagneux[22] and Philippe Gaulier,[23] had left and started their own school, so I also took classes with them. It was two very strong years at the school. Among my classmates were an English writer and director and actor, Simon McBurney,[24] a Canadian, Fiona Gordon, and a Belgian, Dominique Abel.

RA: And Martha, how did you find your way to Paris?

MR: Well, once again, this time in Toronto, I was walking in a blizzard and I saw another little notice for an audition for a play written by Jean Genet, *Deathwatch*, by an all-woman company, directed by a graduate student at the University of Toronto. I'd done a little bit of work with Richard Pochinko[25] as well.

RA: So, you were hanging out in Toronto and taking various classes?

MR: Yeah, then I got the part in the Genet piece, and it was a wonderful experience. The work was very physical, but by the end of the project my money was running out, and I was considering heading home to Vancouver. By chance, I ran into Alan Merovitz, who was hanging lights at the time. Alan said to me, "I know you're not here much longer, but promise me one thing before you go, and that's to take a clown class with Dean Gilmour because he is a genius teacher." Dean had just come back from Paris. It must have been 1979. It was like finding "The Fit"! Dean said: "You know if you can figure out how to get the money, you've got to go to Lecoq." He knew it would be perfect for me. To make a long story short, I went back to the fish plant in BC, made more money, and then went to Lecoq.

RA: That is unique student financing. It was canned salmon that put you through L'École Jacques Lecoq?

MR: Yeah. Funny, huh? I went in 1979-1981, a year before Leah went. I felt perfectly at home, in Paris and at Lecoq. It was almost like I had this feeling that I'd lived in Paris before, although I wasn't fluent in French; I never even got close. I loved the two years there. Yes, it did change my life. Because of the emphasis on creating, it really rang true with me. That is what I'm about. Creation. At Lecoq's school, I was a very much "second year" and Leah was "first year"—there was such snobbism. I thought, "Who is this Canadian who thinks she knows something?" I was jealous and dismissive all at the same time, so Leah was very peripheral. After I graduated, I stuck around France for a few months, then returned to Canada and went back to Vancouver, where I immediately fell into a deep depression.

22 Monica Pagneux, movement teacher at Lecoq's school.
23 Philippe Gaulier, former teacher at L'École Jacques Lecoq, now operaties his own school in London, England.
24 Simon McBurney, actor, director and writer with Theatre de la Complicité in London.
25 Richard Pochinko, teacher, director and influential mentor to many clowns and performance artists across Canada.

RA: Leah and Martha, how did you two meet?

LC: It was totally by chance. We were taking a clown course together taught by Philippe Gaulier, which was organized by Theatre Beyond Words.

RA: Martha, do you recall working with Leah?

Dr. Dapertutto, 1989. Maggie Huculak and Michael Simpson.

MR: It seems to me that within days of Leah returning to Toronto, we had decided that we were going to make a show. Maybe it was a much longer process, but it seems to me much shorter. I was so grateful that this bright light had blown in from Paris that I just embraced her and haven't let go since. You know, I think *Until We Part* is still my most favourite of all the Columbus shows. It was our first creation. We had to waitress, sneak hours here and there. I love that about your late twenties—you can work until five in the morning, smoke and drink and still be ready for rehearsal the next morning. I miss that.

In some ways *Until We Part* was the piece that fulfilled our mandate. There was something absolutely brutal about the central characters, Siamese twins. One would want to go one way and the other would want to go the other way. Then there was our fear of the "outside world," which was falling apart. We had great comic bits; for instance, we were attacked by an electric floor polisher, and at one point my character had to hide her smoking habit from her twin, and we had this thing with an electric fan. It was literally a Buster Keaton relationship with objects.

LC: We created the show with Patsy Nichols. We took eight months to create it. We did the show in a Queen Street office on the third floor and it was full every night…all twenty-five seats. It certainly started the buzz. Then it took us a while to form a company. We did a few projects before we formalized the name, Theatre Columbus.

RA: Were the early years of Theatre Columbus just you and Leah or did you bring in outside collaborators?

MR: Well, we thought it would be great to work with certain people, so we invited them into our process and then the ideas came very organically from the group.

RA: Did you think you could make a living doing this?

LC: Not really. It was really project-to-project. We thought if Columbus could pay us $5,000 a year that would be a good year.

RA: Did you feel that you were actually starting something, finding an audience?

MR: Yeah, it was so organic—we had a great trust that one moment would lead to the next, which would lead to a play, which would lead us to a venue, which would lead us to an audience. There was a wonderful innocence about it, combined with a great trust that somehow it would all work out. It was only in our later years that we started to feel that fear, that panic that comes from being in your forties. You start to mistrust the critics, the audience. Doubt sets in.

RA: We doubt our memory... Well, that's why I thought it was essential to write this book, because in ten years we're not going to remember what happened at all.

LC: In ten years we might not be so full of doubt and distance...we might be rejuvenated again.

RA: You've found a real connection to Leah. What keeps you together? What is the glue?

MR: We really balance each other, our personalities. I write grants, and Leah has this amazing ability to call people and ask for favours; she has no problems with that. She is very clear. So was her discovery that she wanted to direct. I love acting and writing, and she, for the most part, loves directing. Although I think she loves the "holiday" of acting. No responsibilities.

RA: What about your work with Martha, Leah? How has it evolved?

LC: Martha is more "writerly," whereas I've focussed on taking more directing projects. It's collaboration and we trust each other's instincts, and now we both know how to pull out the details in the writing, and we both know how to make the projects happen.

RA: What do you see as your process for creation? What is your particular way of working?

Still, 1994. Martha Ross as Nada. (Photo: Michael Cooper)

LC: As a director, I love to see growth, change. I would say that we just go to the rehearsal hall. I love the environment of rehearsal; I love how work gets created. The work in rehearsal feeds us, and over the years, we've learned to put our trust in the process. I try to create a fine working environment, and of course we place a lot of demands on each other in terms of creative brainstorming. And I'm very aware that the small things are important. Of course we can break the rules so we can find the specific moments and our "method" constantly changes. We have to put our faith and trust in that.

RA: After you started with your show *Until We Part*, which was essentially about you and Martha, when did you start looking for other collaborators, and looking for other sources of inspiration such as new texts and adaptations, which is a different process than showing up in a rehearsal hall with some actors and one good idea?

MR: *Twelfth Night* was our first classical piece, but prior to that we had done something with Crow's Theatre,[26] and a co-production of *The Green Bird* with Smith-Gilmour, and *Infidelity*, a French farce.

RA: In your work, it seems to me that you aren't afraid to take on other writers and text—you keep your process open, rather than being about a particular style or form.

MR: In the early days, I wrote a lot for the company. We were always co-writers, we always threw ideas into the writing pot, and I would always take responsibility to script what was improvised.

LC: Martha would come up with the first draft, so we could springboard from that. Also, she would write knowing who was in the piece. She could script for that particular actor, or give them inspiration to come up with something else.

RA: At the beginning it seems to me you found this energy between you. Did it take a long time before you sought out other sources for inspiration?

LC: Very early on, we started to work with other people. We hired people who were more like us.

MR: In those days it was very balanced…it wasn't like we actively pursued writers, although one writer sought us out. We got talking and he said he would like to write a piece.

LC: Also, we were not interested in doing two-person plays all the time. We had to look around. I think our instinct was to look for something new.

RA: How did you create the hit two-person play *The Anger in Ernest and Ernestine*?

LC: It was completely created through improvisation. At a certain point there was written material for a few scenes.

RA: It was a big hit; the show could have gone on major tours. Did you not think about the commercial viability of touring?

LC: Martha and Robert Morgan[27] couldn't continue doing *The Anger in Ernest and Ernestine*. You know, it took so much out of them. The emotional backdrop and where it all came from. They were both extremely faithful to it, a kernel of something true and real. They did the show three times and even in the last incarnation at The Factory Theatre, they were emotional wrecks, and it wasn't like they had to tap into anything, they just went there. We talked about touring the show all the time, and it never went anywhere, and I think it was because the idea of the emotional strain was in the back of their minds. Maybe we could've found other actors to do it. I've directed other people in it, and other people can do it with less strain. We had Martha and Robert in massage therapy paid for by the company.

RA: Theatre Columbus has not toured its work very much, although productions have been mounted around the world. Did you choose not to tour because of the expense?

LC: Touring just wasn't in the cards, and our sets were always so big, and that made touring pretty impossible. Now, with small kids, it is very tough to leave home for any length of time.

26 Crow's Theatre Company, Toronto-based theatre founded by Jim Millan.
27 Robert Morgan, Toronto-based actor, director and writer.

MR: I also think one of the reasons we haven't gone the route of hiring other actors to take a piece like *Anger* on the road (which is almost to our detriment) is that we just keep coming up with new ideas. It's almost a curse, because it does create restlessness. *Anger* was created in 1986; that is what we were going through then. Perhaps if I had made a company with someone else, I might've followed a different game plan.

RA: Martha, are you in agreement with Leah's assessment of the touring of existing shows versus attending to the creative impulses?

MR: Leah is very good at exploring internal worlds, using the emotional world as a base to build characters within the story. To do that effectively you have to be truthful and you have to keep checking in on yourself. In some ways the raw emotion of *Anger* is always part of our lives, but it was more pertinent then than now.

LC: I believe that we are primarily creators, not actually performers. We love the art of creating. I like performing only because it's easy, so it's a vacation for me. For Martha, the creation is easier. I can see Martha, and she is there working and searching out more details, but it's not the same spark as during the creation process. So, to answer your question, I don't think we'd be happy touring the same show night after night.

Lonely Nights and Other Stories, 2000. Oliver Dennis, Michael Simpson, Martha Ross. (Photo: John Launer)

RA: What are you currently working on?

MR: I'm working as artist-in-residence for the education system, teaching eleven-year-olds about Shakespeare. For the whole year, I'm working in five schools in the city. It was a discovery, via my nephews, that eleven-year-olds have this great instinct for Shakespeare. Better than adults. They have a great sense of the play; they're not afraid of the text, the language. And of course, I am using some of Lecoq's vocabulary on them. They are not daunted at all. They're very perceptive, and can access their imagination, which is probably why I loved Lecoq's teaching; it was so scientific, yet so liberating and so childlike. I had hoped to get back to writing, but haven't found those moments.

RA: Well, you seem to be fully engaged, teaching, plus running a small theatre company.

MR: We are starting something new this year. Leah and I kept talking about this fantasy of having a sabbatical. The company is almost twenty years old, and we need time to ourselves. Time to not write a grant, to not think about fundraising. We took a retreat and thought, why don't we close the office down for six months so we can devote whatever time we need to whatever individual project? So theoretically, the office has been closed, but there are always meetings. The general manager goes in once a week. But it hearkens back to the old days; it's a kind of liberation.

RA: You've been together for twenty years; I think many readers of this book who are in various levels of training would wonder how you keep inspiring yourselves.

LC: It's a really good question.

MR: For one show we decided to do, *Fertility*, we got the idea at the same time but in different parts of the city. The details we had to develop, but the idea was that one woman desperately wants to become pregnant, and the other does not. The woman who doesn't want to get pregnant does. It became a fantastical version of that basic story—it was about an Egyptian Queen and her slave. The ideas for all the shows really do come from different places. For *The Anger in Ernest and Ernestine*, Robert Morgan and Leah were talking one night about experiences with anger...perhaps it was Robert who suggested that it would make a great show. Another show we did in the mid-eighties, *Melancholia*, was my personal obsession inspired by Albert Dürer etchings that I loved—I had a real emotional attachment to this. It was the story of an angel who becomes "grounded" after falling to earth. Sometimes the ideas come from one of us, and sometimes it kind of just evolves. Maybe it is also that we haven't found that show where we say: "This is it!"

LC: You know, the more I think about it, we are like a couple of Beckett characters who are stuck in urns and don't move.

RA: What keeps you together? Do you trust each other's intuition?

LC: I totally trust Martha's intuition.

MR: We laugh at the same things, and we cry at the same things. I wonder if all people who do comedy have this well of sadness...I do know Leah has this. We both have a huge well of sadness, and because of that, we have to do comedy...we're always interested in that exploration.

RA: Is it because you have a loose affiliation, rather than a formal company with a heavy-duty business plan and a touring plan and five-year plans?

LC: In some ways I think that we have not grown up, not matured. Our work has certainly matured, and we have as artists, but as a company, we're still a small theatre company. I'm not sure what that really means. We have just never really bitten the bullet and gotten serious. Perhaps it's been a lack of interest. We've just stuck to creating.

RA: Was there a significant moment in your history of working together as company that was focussed on clown-based work, a point when you felt that you were looking to find an audience, wanting to be seen, to be taken seriously?

MR: There was a significant turning point for our company. We had done a couple of shows at the Poor Alex Theatre, and we were approached by the Crow's Theatre about whether or not we'd be interested in sharing the management of the Poor

Alex Theatre, along with Smith-Gilmour and Crow's Theatre. That was a major change in how we saw ourselves, and our work. It all of sudden became apparent that we'd have a home. Suddenly people started to see us in a different way, with a clear identity. We don't have that now, because we don't have a home.

RA: So the public's perception was that if they went to the Poor Alex, they would see a certain kind of artistic work?

MR: It was called alternative theatre, but there was definitely an audience for that spark that we had. At the Poor Alex we revelled in breaking the "fourth wall." The border between performer and audience was gone. It's interesting, since we've left the Poor Alex, the "fourth wall" has gone mostly up again…and I do miss that complicity, because our work has always been clown-based, looking for the edge.

RA: Leah, you taught at the National Theatre School for years. Are you still focussed on that aspect?

LC: Yes, well, I am teaching at Ryerson right now.

RA: How do you connect with the next wave of actor/creators?

LC: I've been teaching the clown method I devised fifteen years ago, and I still love it, although I do feel the huge gulf between the twenty-one-year-olds and myself. I just keep marvelling at them. I get a kick out of it, returning to it and trying to introduce these ideas of clown to students.

RA: So teaching refreshes you, takes you back to your roots?

LC: I always hope that the students will inspire me.

RA: What kind of advice would you give to the next generation of actors, writers and directors? You have a life, children, and a theatre company…how do you do it?

LC: If I were to tell young people what to do, I'd say that what they are missing right now is experience. They don't have enough experience, life experience. They either haven't yet had enough opportunities to express adult emotions, or tapping into them is very hard. I always think about Lecoq; he didn't admit anyone into his school until they were twenty-one, and that's a huge thing. The students I'm working with now are in third year and they are twenty-one. It's a big difference. By the time I was twenty-one, I'd done a BA, I'd had my own theatre company…you know, I'd already done stuff. And I'd tell them to continue experiencing, go to art galleries and look at stuff, like Martha did, getting inspired by a painting like Albert Dürer's.

MR: Find that freedom to play and search.

LC: Trust your process. Ideas will come. Not just ideas for ideas' sake, but life. Life gives ideas. Work in the theatre can be very satisfying if you allow the actual creation to happen in the rehearsal hall. The process of creation is so dynamic. From that you can create a vocabulary for creation. What is my advice for young artists? Go for help when you need it, go seeking collaborators. With Theatre Columbus we are not socially based or politically driven. We build characters we see around us, characters who are us. For instance, we are currently opening *Lonely Nights and Other Stories*, which are domestic tales and very human dramas.

RA: What other new projects are you working on?

LC: In March 2002 we are doing an adaptation of *Peer Gynt*, called *The Gynty Self*. It has twenty characters and we have five actors, so it's an adaptation. We are using an adaptation by Frank McGuiness. He has already done a lot of cuts, which is a lot of work. It is a surreal radio play, but, for instance, the actors will have to know their lines.

RA: As a company, have you ever thought, "Let's tank this"?

MR: Because we are in our mid-forties and then some, there is that feeling that starts to creep up, like, "How much more can I struggle with budgets?" But we keep going back to it and new material keeps presenting itself. I hope I can do this when I'm sixty.

LC: You know, in some funny ways, it's been a theme of ours right from the beginning: our first show was called *Until We Part*. We've always struggled with the notion of who we are.

We even created a show where we publicly and actively displayed our doubts about the angst about still doing this kind of work; although it was much more of a metaphor. It really is inbred that we will always struggle with those questions.

■ ■ ■

The Anger in Ernest and Ernestine, 1990. Robert Morgan as Ernest, Martha Ross as Ernestine. (Photo: Amir Gavridi)

EXCERPT FROM THE ANGER IN ERNEST & ERNESTINE*

THEATRE COLUMBUS

Ernestine and Ernest enter the kitchen, both dishevelled and agitated.

ERNESTINE: It's ludicrous what they do out there. The government is ludicrous.

ERNEST: We should write a letter. This pen doesn't work.

ERNESTINE: Don't worry about the pen. Just write it.

ERNEST: To whom it may concern…

ERNESTINE: We were nearly killed.

ERNEST: To whom not "it may." To whom it does concern.

ERNESTINE: To whom it does concern!

ERNEST: And I'm going to underline the does!

ERNESTINE: That's good, Ernest. *(Grabbing the pen and paper and writing.)* Underline it three times and put an exclamation mark. We were nearly killed!

ERNEST: To whom it better concern! *(Grabbing the pen back.)*

ERNESTINE: Yeah! To whom it better concern! That's good, Ernest.

ERNEST: To whom it damn well better concern!

ERNESTINE: Yeah, Ernest! Yeah! Or else!

ERNEST: To whom it… *(Pausing.)* To whom it damn well better concern, or else!!

ERNESTINE: Or fuckin' else, Ernest! Fuckin' else!!

ERNEST: Fuckin' else! To whom it damn well better concern or fuck you!!

ERNESTINE: That's good, Ernest! Keep it!!! To whom it fuckin' better concern or fuck off!!!

ERNEST: To whom it…to whom it fuckin' better concern or fuck off…fuck you…

ERNESTINE: Fuck you!

ERNEST: Fuck…fuck off or fuck you?

ERNESTINE: Both!!!

ERNEST: Both. Both!!! To whom it fuckin' better concern or both fuck off and fuck you!!!

ERNESTINE: That's good, Ernest! That's good. Now what's next? We were nearly killed…

ERNEST: No. Oh, no! You nearly killed us!

ERNESTINE: You did!

ERNEST: You did!

ERNESTINE: You tried to kill us!

ERNEST: You did!

ERNESTINE: You…

ERNEST: You…

ERNESTINE: You…

ERNEST: You bastards!

ERNESTINE: Bastards, that's good, Ernest!

ERNEST: Bastards!

ERNESTINE: Bastards!

ERNEST: Bastards!

ERNESTINE: Bastards! Just keep writing, Ernest; we don't want to miss any of the details.

ERNEST: Bastards!

ERNESTINE: The bricks…

ERNEST: Bastards!

ERNESTINE: The kids, the fence, the yelling…

ERNEST: You bastards, fuck off!

ERNESTINE: That's good. Keep it!!!

ERNEST: *(Standing.)* You bastards can fuck right off!!!

ERNESTINE: *(Standing.)* Can fuck right off! You fuckin' bastards can fuckin' fuck right the fuck off!!!

They sit and read to themselves what they have written.

ERNESTINE: Too many fuckin's? *(Pausing.)* Ernest, we only have one life to live and they nearly took it away. Write that down.

ERNEST: I will.

ERNESTINE: No. No. *(Standing, grabbing the letter and putting it in her purse.)* I'm going to tell them. I'm going to go right out there and...

ERNEST: No, don't go out there.

ERNESTINE: I'm going out there because we're sitting here like dodos on a log...

ERNEST: You can't go out there.

ERNESTINE: Ernest, I'm not going to sit here like a dodo on a log.

They collide in front of the table, pushing and shoving like children.

ERNESTINE: I'm—

ERNEST: You can't—

ERNESTINE: Dodo—

ERNEST: Don't go—

ERNESTINE: I'm not— *(Gasping, clapping her hand over her mouth and backing away.)* Ohh, Ernest!

ERNEST: What?

ERNESTINE: Your face.

ERNESTINE: Your facer is squished in...the fence, it...you have an imprint of the fence on your face.

ERNEST: *(Turning his back to the audience.)* Does it look funny? Do I look funny?

ERNESTINE: I still love you, Ernest.

ERNEST: They had no right to put that fence there!

ERNESTINE: Well, you go out there and tell them.

ERNEST: You think I look ugly.

ERNESTINE: You don't look ugly; you just have a face that's a bit squished in.

ERNEST: I have a face that looks like a fence!

ERNESTINE: *(Pausing.)* Ernest, we could sue them!

ERNEST: Those bastards!

They turn and glare at the audience. Black.

■ ■ ■

* Published by Playwrights Canada Press. Reprinted with the permission of the authors.

PRODUCTION HISTORY OF
THEATRE COLUMBUS

2002 **The Gynty Self**
Adapted from Ibsen by Frank McGuiness

2001 **Lonely Nights and Other Stories**
By Leah Cherniak, Oliver Dennis, Maggie Huculak, Martha Ross, Michael Simpson and Ker Wells

2000 **Doubt**
By Michael Redhill with inspiration from the company

1999 **Mayhem and the Naked Muse**
An event celebrating creativity

1998 **The Cherry Orchard**
By Anton Chekhov
Co-production with Theatre Smith-Gilmour

The Betrayal
By Leah Cherniak, Oliver Dennis, Maggie Huculak, Robert Morgan, Michael Simpson and Martha Ross

1996 **The Barber of Seville**
Adapted from Beaumarchais by Michael O'Brien

1995-97 **The Attic, The Pearls, and 3 Fine Girls**
By Jennifer Brown, Leah Cherniak, Ann-Marie MacDonald, Alisa Palmer and Martha Ross

1994 **Knee Plays II**
Collective creation

Still
By Leah Cherniak and Martha Ross

1993 **Ratbag**
By Martha Ross and John Millard

1992 **1492**
By Sean Dixon

The Knee Plays
Collective creation

1991 **Wildlife**
By Diego Matamoros

1990 **Twelfth Night**
By William Shakespeare

1989 **Dr. Dapertutto**
By Martha Ross

Cooking with Columbus
Collective creation

1988 **Paranoia**
By Martha Ross and Theatre Columbus

The Porch People
By Martha Ross

1987 **Turtle Jazz**
By Kevin Teichroeb

The Anger in Ernest and Ernestine
Collective creation

Fertility
Collective creation

1986 **Heartpiece**
By Heiner Müller

1985 **Melancholia**
By Martha Ross and Theatre Columbus

Infidelity
Adapted from *Happiest of the Three* by Labiche

Electrical Wires and other Family Problems
By Kevin Teichroeb

1984 **The Gadi**
Collective creation

Fox Tales
Collective creation

My Dinner with Jerome
By Jim Warren and Theatre Columbus

Until We Part
Collective creation

AXIS THEATRE COMPANY

"We wanted to do something really funny, and thought about contemporary commedia, *whatever that might be. Those were the two main goals that were part of the overall vision. We felt that Melody Anderson's masks were brilliant, and the world of* commedia *was populated with masked characters, so that gave us the base to work from. It was an improv-based process. If we liked it, it stayed in; if we didn't like it, it didn't stay in."*

—WAYNE SPECHT, ARTISTIC DIRECTOR OF AXIS THEATRE

Axis Theatre Company

Wayne Specht is the co-founder and artistic director of Axis Theatre Company in Vancouver, which celebrated its twenty-fifth anniversary in 2001-2002. Wayne, along with Lin Bennett, Elizabeth Murray-Byers and Wendy Gorling, started the company, but, in fact, it is now Wayne who has taken the company from its early roots as a collective mime company to an international touring and mid-sized theatre company. Axis, which shed the word "mime" in its title under Specht's artistic direction, has created an impressive number of original productions since its inception in the 1970s.

Axis Theatre has gone through numerous forms and for many years was touring to schools throughout BC. The company has also produced original mainstage works as part of its mandate, working in collaboration with many writers, such as John Lazarus, Sheldon Rosen and Kim Selody, and with directors such as Arne Zaslove and Roy Surette. Now with the international success of *The Number 14*, which has dizzying performance statistics, the company has been catapulted onto the world stage. The company has received numerous accolades, but more importantly, it has been able to provide almost steady work for the two casts and crews who tour with *The Number 14*. The sheer numbers—over 900 performances and over twenty-one countries toured—for this physical theatre and mask piece is remarkable. The company is now a major employer of physical theatre actors, directors, scenic artists and technicians. Axis Theatre Company now performs regularly in the overseas market—Europe, Australia, Asia and the United States.

Original Company, 1975. Elizabeth Murray-Byers, Lin Bennett, Wayne Specht, Wendy Gorling. (Photo: David Cooper)

Its touring has brought the company to major international festivals, including Edinburgh, where Specht discovered the acrobatic theatre performance troupe Legs-on-the-Wall, a troupe of Australians who have made a mark with their circus-like and gravity-defying performance style. It was a natural collaboration for the character-driven and highly physical Axis team and the more circus-and movement-driven Legs-on-the-Wall.

The resulting new work, a collective creation called *Flying Blind*, is a quad-production involving three Canadian organizations, the Arts Club Theatre, Axis Theatre, The Belfry Theatre, and one Australian company, Legs-on-the-Wall. The Belfry's artistic director, Roy Surette, acts as the director for the entire project. This project recently had its Canadian premiere at the Arts Club Theatre and will be travelling to Sydney, Australia with hopes of repeating the route taken by *The Number 14*.

The Number 14 is the defining piece for Axis Theatre and its great tradition of creating physical theatre and comic "mime" plays. Most striking is the simplicity of the structure—an urban bus picks up the city's strays, oddballs and lunatics, its aged, and its young—by the time the two-hour performance has come to an end, the Number 14 has picked up just about every kind, size, age and ethnic group in humanity, all heading to some "destination," to bingo, a school outing to look at spiders, to work, even to nowhere. The comic energy is wonderful to watch. Artistic director and founder Wayne Specht appeared in *The*

Number 14, playing an overfed kid, a fish plant worker and a nervous passenger. Wayne informed me during our interview that he has since retired from performing with the touring companies, but his keen sense of comic business and detailed mask work is very evident throughout the sketches.

The performance style is raucous, fun, engaging and highly entertaining. It features beautiful masks made by Vancouver-based mask maker Melody Anderson, and the company of acrobatic and physical actors engage their wacky masked characters with great bravado. The broad comic strokes are certainly a homage to the Charlie Chaplinesque style of clowning, with love-lorn and estranged couples colliding into each other as the bus leaves each stop. There is also plenty of raunchy humour, with life's-most-embarassing-moments-while-riding-on-the-bus gags, flatulence jokes, snot mischief and brilliantly performed pratfalls.

Colin Heath, the Vancouver-based clown and acrobatic actor, is hilarious to watch, particularly when he portrays a little old lady. As the bus takes off over and over, Heath's ease with tumbling and bar hanging creates a stupendous effect, which for a moment turns the stationary bus into a moving circus, as he tumbles from seat to seat, into the rails, and as the finale of this "number," tumbles up into the trolley wires and electrocutes himself. Heath also plays a drunken slob, who slimes the entire bus, in contrast to Peter Anderson's flower-hugging, zany clean freak. The two characters wind up in a battle of wills, a bus riders' pas-de-deux, tumbling through the bars and thc scats looking for free space and finally an exit.

The focus is on fun, with a dose of subversive humour, frequently supplied by the West Coast-based comic actor Peter Anderson. His rap-man song, which ends the first act, is subversion personified. The pièce de résistance, however, is Anderson's lunatic hippie character, a character who defies description—a kind of town crier, sermon-from-the-mount soothsayer, faith healer, news collector, shaman, wise man, and just all-round crazy man who turns the whole show on its head. He declares to the audience that, "It is nuts for paying close to thirty dollars to watch half a bus that is going nowhere." It is a sublime subversion, and this is where the show becomes more dramatic and very interesting, as the masked characters jostle and struggle to subdue the "truth-teller." When the struggle ends, it is make-believe that triumphs.

Behind all the zaniness is the brilliant work of the composer, Doug McCauley. The musical score is a playful and evocative backdrop to the manic action as the bus stops and goes. This finely tuned balance of terrific music, finely honed physical comedy, detailed mask work, rousing acrobatics, and sharply defined character work can play anywhere.

The best description for this work is actually the title itself., "number," as in clown number. The numbers are tailor-made for the team of acrobat and physical actors; each one of them brings a zany and comic element. The cast plays what seems like an army of characters during the two-hour performance, and the fun seems to spill into everything and everywhere the bus stops.

Axis Theatre has become the closest thing in Western Canada to the Cirque du Soleil, particularly now, with its strong focus on working with acrobatic actors, such as the Australians in *Flying Blind* and the dynamic comedic actors who will literally climb the walls for the company. It is wonderful to witness the success of the company. Wayne's commitment to the art of original creation of comic, imagistic theatre and text-based theatre certainly has touched many lives on the west coast, and of course now, the world.

■ ■ ■

RA: Wayne, I've been speaking with many of your former colleagues, such as Robin Patterson and Harro Maskow, and I'd like to start this interview by talking about the early years at the Canadian Mime Theatre. How did you find out about this company?

WS: Many years ago, I was a starving actor living in Toronto. I went down to the Equity office, and saw a notice that Canadian Mime Theatre was doing auditions for a show that was to be done up in Ottawa. I went home and told my wife that I was going to become a mime.

RA: So you were not watching Marcel Marceau and said, "This is what I want to be"?

WS: Well, I had already done something with Wendy Gorling and Robin Patterson in BC. In fact, Robin and I had already made a company.

RA: Was this Troupe of the Seasons at Simon Fraser University?

WS: Yeah, with Robin. We performed on the beaches around Vancouver. We had as much dope in our hat as money.

The Number 14, 1994. Colin Heath, Peter Anderson, Beatrice Zeillenger, David Mackay, Darlene Brooks, Allan Zinyk. (Photo: David Cooper)

Flying Blind, 2001. Debra Iris Batton, Peter Anderson. (Photo: Tim Matheson)

RA: Pretty wild beginnings.

WS: I certainly had the background and the training from my time at the National Theatre School. In fact, Arne Zaslove[28] was and still is my mentor from my time there. Anyway, I auditioned and one week later we were in Ottawa doing a show called *The Lamplighter*. It was a mime play, not vignettes. It was probably in 1969 or so.

RA: These were the very early years of this expression called mime. Nobody really knew what it was. When I was talking with Harro Maskow, he originally had no idea about the form. In fact, he was in art school when somebody suggested he should try this mime thing. Did you think that it was important that you were bringing this art form to the world?

WS: Yeah, we were certainly aware of the newness, although it has ancient roots, perhaps the oldest in Western theatre traditions. At the time, Marceau was definitely out there as the leader. He created visibility and excitement. Even the American artists like Shields and Yarnell[29] had a great influence on the general awareness of the art form through more visible media like television.

RA: When you started with Canadian Mime Theatre, were you part of the original creations, or did you fill in?

WS: I was in their vignette shows—there was existing material, which we created together. Then I started adapting and directing some of the kids' shows like *Pinocchio*, and worked for the company for a couple of years.

RA: The stories from this time period really do speak about freedom that younger artists have no idea about. From your perspective as a producer and director, where do you feel the people of this generation coming up can get work?

WS: I look back on my own experience; I tried to find work as an actor. I knew I had good physical skills, and it was a good fit at the time. I was the young energetic guy, and Adrian and Harro were a little older. In fact, Adrian's kids were all grown up by the time I started at the Canadian Mime Theatre. He had had a long career as an accountant before the mime

28 Arne Zaslove, mime teacher, actor and former artistic director of Bath House Theatre in Seattle, Washington.
29 Shields and Yarnell. American mime duo had a popular television show in the 1970s. They studied with American master teacher, Tony Montanaro.

career. For me, it was really lucky timing to get those three years of experience. Then I went to Lecoq's school. I had already toured extensively with the company, and to tell you the truth, I was getting tired of the vignette format. I was interested in playwriting and in telling a story, which was more my background from my time at the National Theatre School. So, I wrote to Lecoq and asked him if I could come and create a playwriting program within the school. He agreed and I went for three months and worked on how to tell a story physically, and even how to write and notate all the actions and intentions. I never really succeeded. I concluded later that a scenario or outline is the best you're going to get before the rehearsal process. It's too hard on the imagination to note all the movements in advance for live theatre. It doesn't allow for the actors' impulses. I did learn that I could notate, although I found it boring myself, so I imagined others would find it boring as well. It was good refresher, considering I had learned many of the principles that Arne Zaslove had taught at the NTS. Lecoq liked me; he actually knew my name, which was rare. He used to say: *"Pas mal, Specht, pas mal!"* It was hard to leave Lecoq's school, but that was the plan and that was my budget. I returned to Toronto and starved a bit. Then one of my brothers died while in China so I returned to the coast. I resettled in Vancouver and was doing bits and pieces, here and there. Then I was invited by Wendy Gorling, Elizabeth Murray-Byers and Lin Bennett to work on their show as a director.

RA: Wayne, before we speak about Axis Theatre, I'd like to ask you about the Canadian Mime Theatre. Were you there during the whole financial and artistic meltdown?

WS: I was there when they did the first season at the Royal George Theatre. I remember my last season there. I was really exhausted. Harro was adapting *Seven Deadly Sins* and there was a student company component developing, which was an apprenticeship programme. We workshopped that piece, which in the end became a very cool play. It was enlightening and refreshing for everybody because it was an artistic stretch for the regular members of the company. They had fallen into a pattern of vignette work. It was about that time that Adrian and Harro started to have problems. Then I left the company to go to Lecoq's school, and by the time I came back, the company was in turmoil. They had brought in Wayne Pritchard around that time to run the school. Ray Wickens played a big role as the founding GM. When it all blew up, Adrian quit and Harro quit, and Pritchard was left adrift. The company folded and was literally thrown out on the street. It was pretty messy. This all happened while I was away in France. I think the mime school actually survived for six or seven more years before being shut down.

RA: All the artists I've interviewed left the country for their training, and then many came back to perform and teach. The sad fact is that there is no formal training now for the next generation. Is mime is dead? Gone? Kaput?

WS: There is no mime as we knew it then. Particularly illusion mime—but there is non-verbal theatre like our company performs and certainly all the clown-esque elements of the form, which artists like Martha Ross and Leah Cherniak, for example, have incorporated. In fact, it has been Canadian artists who have diversified the form and pushed the limits of the ancient traditions. That is great.

RA: Do you think that the wind has gone from the sails for physical theatre training?

WS: Well, we are lucky here on the Coast; we have Wendy Gorling, who is probably the best teacher of physical theatre in Canada. When she went to teach at Studio 58 at Langara College it created a perfect situation for people like me, in that the students get wonderful acting training and strong physical theatre training. Many of them graduate with amazing skills, and I hire them. It's an ideal situation. Kathryn Shaw, who runs the theatre department, loves physical theatre, and Wendy is able to really instill a passion for the art form. Kathryn has been very supportive of Wendy and her work. There are small pockets of influence across the country: Ralph Allison at Concordia University, Paul Wilder at the University of Toronto, Deborah Cottreau at the University of Saskatchewan, and Jan Henderson at the University of Alberta. They are out there. The other influential teacher of the Lecoq method was Ron East,[30] who recently moved to

30 Ron East now has a school of physical theatre in London, England.

London, England. He set up his school there and has an international student body. I recently visited him and he has a wonderful studio.

RA: Training in this art form seems more based on finding particular teachers at institutions than seeking out the master teachers. Would you recommend attending Lecoq School even though Lecoq himself passed away a couple of years ago?

WS: I would say check the teachers, their reputation. The founder is not there any more, and times change. All of the great teachers have left. There are others, like Desmond Jones[31] in London; he has had a school for years.

RA: When you are auditioning actors for your shows, are you looking only for physical skills, or are you casting for characters? What do you need?

WS: I guess it's both. It is based on need. In Vancouver, the majority of young actors are coming out of Studio 58. I can expect that they will have this background and vocabulary for physical theatre expression. I used to find actors from the University of Victoria because of Kaz Pietkowitz. He is retired, although Brian Richmond is now head of the programme at U Vic and he has a strong passion for this work as well. Of course, Sherry Bie, who worked in the early days of the Canadian Mime Theatre, is now the head of acting at the National Theatre School, so in a few years we should be seeing her influence on the next generation.

RA: In the early days, many companies toured across the country—as you did—inspiring audiences. How does this translate into developing artists who want to work in this way?

WS: In order for the art form to survive, it has to travel, much like modern dance companies have to travel, because there is a finite audience for the art form. It is rare that a show finds popular acceptance and can run for extended periods in cities. *The Number 14* played for over nine months in Vancouver and that's a lot of shows in this city. But that is a real exception; it became its own phenomenon. And it's so strongly rooted in the style. To come back to the travelling aspects, the irony continues to hold true; for example, *The Number 14* had much greater success here after it went away and received great reviews in New York...

RA: Ah, the crazy world of endorsement.

WS: They liked it in New York; therefore, it must be good.

RA: I'd like to talk about the creation of *The Number 14,* and about working with the director, Roy Surette.[32] What was your role in particular? Were you more a writer?

WS: I was an equal creative partner with everybody.

RA: So from inspiration to rehearsal, what is the process? Were the masks built first?

WS: We wanted to do something really funny, and thought about contemporary *commedia*, whatever that might be. Those were the two main goals that were part of the overall vision. We felt that Melody Anderson's masks were brilliant, and the world of *commedia* was populated with masked characters, so that gave us the base to work from. It was an improv-based process. If we liked it, it stayed in, if we didn't like it, it didn't stay in.

RA: How long was the process of finding the show?

WS: We went through several stages of one- or two-week workshops. We even had Arne Zaslove come in and work with us...it was fantastic. We did that because the creative people in the room had different vocabularies—we had a cast from theatre, circus, and pure clown traditions. We had a student of mine from UBC, Peter Anderson, who had his a training from the Dell'Arte School[33] in California, and Colin Heath, who is an acrobat. Arne gave us a brilliant couple of days; it was a significant reminder to us of the rules of getting to the fourth level and staying there. When you have that, you can go anywhere.

RA: So the development of *The Number 14* was a fairly long process?

31 Desmond Jones runs the Desmond Jones School of Mime and Physical Theatre based in England.
32 Roy Surette is the artistic director of the Belfry Theatre in Victoria, BC.
33 The Dell'Arte School, which is based in Blue Lake, California, features physical theatre training. Founded by Carlo Clementi-Mazzone.

WS: It was about a month of workshopping, then a three-week rehearsal period.

RA: Did you capture any of the rehearsal process on tape?

WS: Unfortunately, no.

RA: The musical score is really evocative. Who was the composer?

WS: I found an amazing composer, Doug McCauley, who had worked with the Montreal-based contemporary dance company, La La La Human Steps.

RA: How long have you been touring the show?

WS: This is the ninth year, and we are closing in on nine hundred performances.

RA: Does each cast shape their character work for the show?

WS: Well, it did go through a bit of an evolution. We stayed with the original six cast members for quite a while, then Gina Bastone left the company, and then we recast as required. The show itself went through some of the necessary evolutionary process. When we pay the royalties, we also pay the new creators in addition to the original six co-creators.

Hotsy Totsy, 1979. Michael Miller, Gordon White, Wendy Gorling, Annie Wright, Michael Taylor, Wayne Specht, Elizabeth Murray-Byers. (Photo: David Cooper)

Over the years, the play has had about twenty-five different people perform in the show, and the piece has become very set. New actors bring new energy, but once it got up to the level of five hundred performances, there was cause for celebration when a new gag could be jammed in somewhere, because the show was so tight. There are changes for touring dates and language. For example, on the recent tour that we did to Europe, we went to Northern Italy, which in fact was a German-speaking audience, and then we went to Helsinki, where they spoke English, and then we went to Denmark, where the audience spoke some English, but mostly Danish. It required us to rethink how we were going to present the show, plus we performed it outdoors at two different festivals, and this was really the first time ever we really had to change some of the sketches. What is amazing is that the cast had performed it at least one hundred times, so they could go into it themselves and make changes—like, we just don't need to say that line here. As a matter of fact, the changes to the sketches with the reduction of the text improved the piece. We've recently had a request to take the show to São Paulo in Brazil, and the organizer has tremendous interest in the show, but wondered if it would be possible to put some Brazilian musicians into the show…an interesting possibility. I sent him back an e-mail, asking him what he imagined for this.

RA: So do you think about translation when you are performing overseas?

WS: When we toured to Japan, we took a lot of the English out and replaced it with Japanese. The audience loved it. We also did that with somewhat less success with Finnish and Danish, and have done it with Italian and German, so the cast has to be on top of it.

RA: Where do you feel the show has had the strongest response?

WS: Hong Kong. They went crazy for the show. We gave only four performances there, but the audiences were astonishing.

RA: Are there lessons to be learned for Canadian artists who take their work across borders?

WS: Well, I think it certainly is terrific for the career of the show and it gives Canadian artists a window to see the world, as well as giving international audiences a window into Canadian theatre. It also gave me a better perspective on the local arts scene in Vancouver and how Axis fits into that picture. And without international touring, I would not have met Legs-on-the-Wall Theatre and pursued this international collaboration. Now we have built *Flying Blind* in two countries, Australia and Canada, bringing some incredibly talented people together. The show is very unique; it's a fusion of European-style clowning with an Australian/Canadian sensibility. The show is good. It does have problems, but someday, if we are allowed to move it forward, as *The Number 14* got to move forward, it's going to be stunning. It's really different.

RA: Do you use the rehearsal period for touring to revise and rewrite? Is this a plan for the latest work?

WS: For sure. We've actually left the set here in Vancouver to make technical adjustments. Then we will ship it to Sydney. It's a huge project. I'd like to see another four-week rehearsal period before it's complete. We will see… It's a big company—four Australians and four Canadians.

RA: Many productions in this country never make it past the initial mounting. The creation and process of putting it all together is clearly understood, but the second production seems virtually impossible to attain. How do you do it, admit to what is missing and have the courage to make the adjustment?

WS: By admitting what have we learned. Then we continue to build and live with a show that goes through all the stages. The show has a real career.

RA: That's very interesting; it seems to go against the professional Canadian theatre model of rehearsal and performance.

WS: Yes, Canadian theatre mostly follows the pattern of put it together, do it for a few weeks, then throw it away.

RA: Would you say that this style of work is still coming in the back door of the theatres, as a kind of freak show, with masks and no playwright? Many artists have struggled, because the perception is that mime, storytelling, clown and physical theatre are derivative. But on the other hand, the play, the theatricality and the humour seem to say that if it's a terrific show, it can go just about anywhere.

WS: Well, it is nudging more onto the mainstage here in Vancouver. The Playhouse producing *The Overcoat*, and the Arts Club presenting *The Number 14* and co-producing *Flying Blind* is significant. The whole project was a quad-pro. The Arts Club was really committed to the show; we just ran for five weeks as its first show of the season. The show will go back to the Arts Club in a year or two. This is certainly because of Bill Millard and his awareness that if he just presents traditional plays, and stands still, he and his audience will wither. I really like the fact that he is saying to us, "Here is my audience. Why don't you stretch them a little bit?" That is exactly what is happening.

■ ■ ■

Flying Blind, 2001. Alexandra Harrison (on wall), Brendon Shelper. (Photo: Tim Matheson)

PRODUCTION HISTORY OF
AXIS THEATRE

2001/02 **Flying Blind**
Lois Anderson, Peter Anderson, Debra Iris Batton, Manon Beaudoin, Alexandra Harrison, Colin Heath, Veronica Neave, Carl Polke, Brendan Shelper, Roy Surette

Mouse
Clem Martini

The Number 14

2000/01 **The Number 14**

Crusoe

The Field

1999/00 **Wreck Beach**
David Rhymer

The Number 14

Robinson Crusoe

The Field
Clem Martini

1998/99 **Robinson Crusoe**
Colin Heath

The Number 14

1997/98 **Friends**
Kim Selody, Wayne Specht, Gordon White

Great Canadian Train Comedy
Laura DiCicco, Neil Gallagher, Tom Jones

1996/97 **For Arts' Sake**
Colin Heath

Disposing of the Dead
Kate Schlemmer

1995/96 **Trolldom: As If By Magic**
Asya Pavlovic, Sean Phillips, Heidi Specht

Rhythm in Theatre
Vancouver Moving Theatre

Oliver Sudden's Instant Circus
Colin Heath

1994/95 **The Number 14**

Hopes, Dreams, and Wishes
Michelle Porter, Wayne Specht

1993/94 **The Number 14**

Lost Feeling
Kim Selody

1992/93 **Not Just Junk**
Wayne Specht, Michael Wolski

The Number 14
Melody Anderson, Peter Anderson, Gina Bastone, Colin Heath, David Mackay, Wayne Specht, Roy Surette, Beatrice Zeilinger

1991/92 **Wild Rose and Half a Step**
Robert Stelmach

1990/91 **Hot Times**
David Bloom

1989/90 **Spud the Amazing**
Wayne Specht, Michael Wolski

The Comix Tale
Wayne Specht

1988/89 **The Invisible Man**
Steve Petch

1987/88 **Bodyworks**
Teri Snelgrove

Identical Islands
John Lazarus

1986/87 **Sign Posts**
Louis Smadbeck

1985/86 **Via Rail Pavilion Show (Expo '86)**

Synthetic Energy
Kim Selody

Beaux Gestes '86

1984/85 **Play It Safe**
Kim Selody, Wayne Specht, Gordon White

Who Was That Masked Man?
Gloria Latham

1983/84 **Peter and the Wolf**
Adapted by Wayne Specht

Beginnings
Gloria Latham

Only Birds and Fools Fly
Kim Selody

1982/83 **Fools' Angel**
Kim Selody

1981/82 **Once Upon a Mime**
Gloria Latham

1980/81 **Mime Fest '80**

Elwood's Electrifying Experience
Axis ensemble

1980/81 **Impact**
Sheldon Rosen

1979/80 **Friends**
Kim Selody, Wayne Specht, Gordon White

Rude Awakening
Kim Selody, Wayne Specht, Gordon White

1978/79 **BC Days**
Elizabeth Murray-Byers

Hotsy Totsy
Dennis Foon, Brian Richmond, Humphrey and the Dumptrucks

1977/78 **Hugo's Dream**
Elizabeth Murray-Byers, Wayne Specht, Gordon White

Heracles
Denis Foon

Dwelling
Sheldon Rosen

Mime Over Matter
Wendy Gorling, Elizabeth Murray-Byers, Wayne Specht, Gordon White

1976/77 **Tinder Box**
Adapted by Wayne Specht

Mime Zone
Lin Bennett, Wendy Gorling, Elizabeth Murray-Byers, Wayne Specht

WENDY GORLING

"I can teach you to be funny, but I want you to be able to turn on a dime, so that the audience is still expecting that, and then all of a sudden, it's not funny anymore, and then you grab them, because that is what life is all about. It's easy to do, if you find the heart, the care and the real vulnerability, and what I mean by vulnerability is simply the honesty, admitting that, in fact, you are not the most important person in the world."

—WENDY GORLING, MASTER TEACHER IN PHYSICAL THEATRE

Wendy Gorling

> "I am nobody. I am a neutral point through which you must pass in order to articulate your own theatrical voice. I am only there to put obstacles in your path, so that you can find a better way around them."[34]
>
> —Jacques Lecoq

The Overcoat, 2000. Morris Panych, Paul Moniz de Sa, Peter Anderson, Wendy Gorling, Susan McFarlan. (Photo: David Cooper)

There are very few master teachers who can embody these words of Lecoq's, let alone translate them into actual teaching practice. Wendy Gorling, a teacher of the essential theatre forms, is certainly one of them. A former student of Lecoq herself, she is now an ardent and passionate teacher of clown, tragedy, mask, *commedia dell'arte*, movement and acting at the Studio 58 Theatre School in Vancouver. For many artists, particularly on the west coast of Canada, she is an important theatre teacher, movement coach and collaborator. Most recently she has begun a series of unique collaborations with the Vancouver playwright Morris Panych. Their latest work, the stage and television adaptation of Nikolai Gogol's *The Overcoat,* was a huge success. This ambitious work, which was originally mounted at the Vancouver Playhouse, has toured to Winnipeg, Toronto, and Ottawa, where it was well received. Tours were planned overseas, but ran into the classic Canadian conundrum: lack of money to take a large and expensive show abroad.

34 Jacques Lecoq, in an interview with Simon McBurney. From the Introduction of *The Moving Body.*

I was not able to see the original stage production, but Wendy invited me to see the premiere screening of the teleplay at the Tinseltown Cinemas when I was in Vancouver. This teleplay adaptation, originally produced at the Playhouse Theatre with a large cast of twenty-two, included both professional and student actors, all trained by Wendy Gorling. The teleplay version was a co-production of CBC TV, Radio-Canada, Principia and Rhombus Media. The entire production for television was directed by Morris Panych. One of the things that makes this television adaptation so unique is the underlay of evocative music of Shostakovich's jazz suites and concertos. For the television version, the CBC Vancouver Orchestra performed under the direction of Mario Bernardi. The quality of the work and sheer exuberance of the company, combined with Gorling's and Panych's eerie vision, give the teleplay a feel of early Soviet-style film in the vein of Sergei Eisenstein.[35] The punctuated and driving movement was carefully conceived by Gorling, and brought to life under Panych's fine direction.

The central character, a draughtsman known simply as The Man, is played by rubber-faced and spaghetti-legged Peter Anderson. He is pathetic, industrious, and ultimately tragic. He fantasizes about conceiving his most elegant object ever, the overcoat. As The Man, Anderson plays all the notes made available to him. Panych sets the piece in a madhouse, and this metaphor brilliantly resonates throughout the teleplay.

In the teleplay, Wendy Gorling is cast as the landlady, who, in attempt after attempt, tries to seduce the draughtsman. She is funny, dirty and grotesque. Gorling's physical comedic ability and depth of character reveal her profound understanding of what it takes to create engaging, funny characters who are, in fact, tragic at the core. The old woman's sexual desperation is played with great timing as a counterpoint to Anderson's maniacally perfectionist character who has only one obsession, the luxurious overcoat.

Choreography and movement exactly synchronized to the music are certainly the essence of this work, yet the entirely wordless adaptation nonetheless evokes and honours Gogol. The essential story of desire and hopelessness remains and is punctuated by many sharply defined and moving scenes. The story is particularly poignant when the overcoat is stolen by gaudy whores, and the ending is nothing short of tragic. The man has lost his coat and retreats into the madhouse—and into complete irrelevance.

At the end of the screening, as the lights snap back on, the cast and many members of the orchestra erupt in applause for this visually beautiful and ultimately heartbreaking work. I meet Wendy at the screening, and we arrange for the interview the following day.

I arrive at an attractively renovated old house where workmen are digging at the foundation to repair a basement leak, which can be a major disaster in Vancouver during the rainy months. Wendy Gorling invites me in to her home, which she shares with her photographer husband and teenaged daughter.

Gorling has taught the Lecoq-based style at Studio 58 at Langara College in Vancouver for twenty-three years. She has a reputation for being a blunt and demanding master teacher—something she is aware of—but the paradox is, I find her warm and generous, an exacting seeker and questioner. Wendy has found a real place to teach from, combining the most essential qualities of the teacher of theatre: honesty and precision, along with an uncompromising eye. She seeks the artist in her students.

Gorling speakes eloquently and passionately about theatre training, her work as an artist and her collaboration with Morris Panych on their latest project, *The Overcoat*. She is frank, very funny and serves a wickedly good cup of tea.

■ ■ ■

35 Sergei Eisenstien, Russian filmmaker, famous for his landmark film, *Battleship Potemikin.*

RA: Where did you receive your training?

WG: A theatre group in high school got me interested in theatre. Then I went on to university, dropped it and went into English. I was in the process of doing an honours English class, and was getting pretty independent and frustrated about putting all my energy into a typewriter. I had met this really nice lady in my English class, Robin Patterson. It was Robin Patterson who was my first mime teacher; she was a wonderful teacher. Then the Canadian Mime Theatre came to play at SFU and Harro Maskow gave us a workshop in neutral mask. Anyway, something twigged in me and I decided I should go and study this art form as well. So Robin and I ended up in Paris at the same time.

RA: You were obviously inspired by the exposure to Canadian Mime Theatre. Did you feel that by studying at Lecoq's famous school you would find out what it was to be a mime and an actor?

WG: I thought I was going to France to learn illusion mime, but when I got there, I was shocked to find out that the illusion mime course was for only two hours out of the week. What I discovered at the school was that the other stuff we were learning was so much more important than illusion mime. We were doing mask work, understanding psychological energy, and all the abstract work.

RA: So, in fact, the school and Lecoq's pedagogy opened a lot of new doors.

WG: I'll always remember one of the teachers saying, "I know you can open a door mimetically. Stop showing off! Let's get on with the work." The work, believing in the dramatic situation, and using the illusion to be able to fully source your creativity—that's what we did through all the different styles, through animals, the elements, and so on. So everything that was suggested was a shock to me.

RA: The anglophone artists I've spoken to who studied at the school mentioned that language was a problem at the school. It seems to me that must have been a shock. Did you speak enough French to understand the classes?

WG: I always had my dictionary, and I was continually looking up words. It was very humbling because we (anglophones) couldn't really understand the critique that was given to us. So there would often be someone who would translate. In the end, not knowing French actually became an advantage, because I had to really watch, and I had to make assumptions about what was strong or not strong and then see if that was what Monsieur Lecoq was saying. I couldn't be lazy.

RA: I've spoken to a lot of people who went to the school, and I find it interesting, this choice of leaving the safety of your own country and flying to Europe to study a pretty marginal and European art form. It's a risk. At the conclusion of your studies, did you want to stay in Europe and form a new company?

WG: That was a possibility. I had wanted to go back and work as a shepherdess in Switzerland, between the first and second year, but then my mother died and I returned to Canada. What can I say? I think I was handed to the right people. Someone gave me a number to contact Elizabeth Ball at Carousel Theatre. She was head of the Arts Club summer school, which later became the Carousel summer school, and she was intrigued about what I had just come from. She said to me, "You have to teach." I told her, "I'm sorry, I have no idea what I would teach. I am not a teacher. I'm a performer."

Clowns at École Jacques Lecoq, 1973. Robin Patterson and Wendy Gorling.

She was adamant; she threw me in. So within a year of leaving the Lecoq school, I was teaching what I had just learned.

RA: At the time, were you working with Wayne Specht and Axis Mime Theatre?

WG: I had worked with Wayne before in Vancouver. What happened was, I had started teaching at Carousel, then Tamanhous Theatre brought me in to do workshops for professional actors and I met Kathryn Shaw. Tamanhous was organizing a women's theatre festival. Also at the that time, Lin Bennett came into town, and then another "Lecoqian," Elizabeth Murray-Byers, moved to Vancouver. Then we heard that Wayne Specht had moved back to Vancouver. We contacted him and asked if he would direct us for the women's festival. Wayne agreed and it was a lovely success. The show was a series of mime sketches. It was an event. Certainly mime wasn't being done, so a lot of people came. We thought, "This is very interesting. Why don't we start a company?" That's how Axis Mime Theatre got started.

RA: Did you run it as a collective?

WG: At the beginning, but Wayne was more or less at the head. You know, I don't actually recall when, but at some point we started to get angry at each other. I was asked to leave the company. At any rate, I was starting to get interested in other forms of theatre, particularly as a result of my connection to Elizabeth Ball, who had started me out with teaching. She had the children's theatre company and pushed me into being one of her lead actresses in the seventies and early eighties.

RA: So in fact, your stint with Axis Mime Theatre was short-lived.

WG: I kept working with Axis, but more on a project basis. And you know, in retrospect, I think Axis was ahead of its time doing mime plays and non-verbal plays, in particular *Impact*, a play written by Sheldon Rosen[36] and directed by Peter Froelich.[37] It was spectacular, with very high production values. Another project, *Hotsy Totsy*, had Humphrey and the Dumptrucks doing the narrative.

RA: Did you see yourself as more peripheral?

WG: I got interested in directing. I co-directed a couple of their plays; one play was called *Beginnings*, which was a mask play. I also built the masks. I was also a mask maker. I still teach mask-making to students. I was getting curious about other forms of theatre, not only non-verbal. So, in fact, my curiosity led me away from the company. My teaching became more important. I wanted to spread my wings a little bit.

RA: The idea of starting a group based on a particular form or style seems very passé. Do you think current students of theatre have any desire to build on the ideas and aesthetics of what groups like Axis started so many years ago, or is that idea dead?

WG: I think it's partially a question of money. How can they form a new group when existing groups are disbanding because they are not getting money from the Canada Council? And they have to go into small theatres that are in places where no audience wants to go. And to rent a theatre is so expensive. They just don't have the capital to start it up. When we were starting up Axis Mime Theatre we had the possibility of youth grants like the LIP[38] grants. It wasn't that hard to get money. It was a struggle, but today it's more like a mountain of a struggle.

RA: You have been teaching for many years. From your experience, what do you think Lecoq was looking for in his pedagogy?

WG: What Lecoq tried to do with each individual was to find his or her artistry, and challenge his or her artistry. "What do you want to say as an artist? What do want to say as a performer? Here is the style. What can you do with the style?" Certainly with *commedia dell'arte*,[39] we were told not to go to the library to read up about it. He insisted that we experience it. It had to reverberate for each individual. The strength of

36 Sheldon Rosen, playwright now teaching at Ryerson College, Toronto.
37 Peter Froelich, now a professor in the theatre department at the University of Ottawa.
38 LIP (Local Initiatives Program) and OFY (Opportunities for Youth) were government grants to youth and arts groups during the Trudeau years.
39 Commedia dell'arte, Italian-broad slapstick comedies featuring stock masked characters, such as Arlechinno and Pantelone.

that approach was that when we finished school we could make our own theatre creations. We were curious and rebellious. So in fact, it was very non-intellectual, very experiential. As performers, we didn't have an intellectual base. All we could do was do it, try something. The result was that we became very empowered by Lecoq's methods.

RA: You've gone through many collaborations and built a body of work, now pretty intensively with Morris Panych, and you're teaching permanently at Studio 58—is this the *métier* that you've established?

WG: As a true "Lecoqian," I would say everything I do is focussed on the act of creation. I keep my foot in all things, and that's what gives me most pleasure. I think it's very, very important to pass on my knowledge. That's an important aspect of my career.

RA: I sense that you are very connected to teaching. Is that right?

WG: I'm very passionate about it. What I always make my students understand is that we are dealing with my creativity and we are dealing with their creativity. The important questions must be asked, "What do you have to say as an artist?" "Does this really satisfy what you are doing, or is there more?" In the second year, I teach character mask, so that they understand the principles of *lazzi*,[40] and how to take physical business and play with it as much as they can, and an understanding of cutting the fourth wall. Then taking what they think might be comedy, and switching it into drama, so that there is a "heart" connection. What I am finishing off with right now in the second semester is *pantomime blanche*, where they have to do gesture language, so when they go into the third semester, they have to do more movement. For example, they have to know how to move in period costumes from different eras for particular plays. I teach them to understand "elegance" in their bodies.

RA: Studio 58 places a real emphasis on the physical training. What you describe seems very different in its approach to actor formation.

Imaginary Invalid, 1996. Wendy Gorling as Monsieur Fleurant. (Photo: David Cooper)

40 *Lazzi* or *l'azzione* provides the basic opportunity for playfulness in the *commedia dell'arte* scenarios. Very different from a gag, which can be mechanical or absurd, whereas *lazzi* always has a human reference.

The Overcoat, 2001 television production. Wendy Gorling as The Landlady. (Photo: David Cooper)

WG: It's very European in that way. In the first semester they have three classes of movement, and two classes in alignment. So the students get to look at all their own alignment problems by watching themselves on video, as well as doing a lot of inner work. They can take that into the second semester as well.

RA: Were you involved in designing this programme?

WG: Kathryn Shaw really understands what I am doing, and she helped incorporate it. In the second semester I do a course called The Power Song. The students have to create a song with a melody. The song is about their own power and who they are, what they've become, and how they can sit at the centre of their existence, and say, "Here I am as an artist." They have class once a week, and they have to choreograph it, and eventually we put all the songs together and create either a play or a presentation.

RA: Does all this teaching and mentoring inform your own performing and directing?

WG: It's always a test to see if what I am teaching works, to see if what I am saying can hold. What do I do? What do I say? As a performer, I must decide whether my character has an element of fire, water, earth, air, or whether my character lives in the nervous system, or the muscle system, or another organ system. As a teacher, I must speak about character work, as it is central to all the teaching; it's really character work that my acting work is based on. No one ever recognizes me on stage, because I look so different. The students must learn how to totally immerse themselves—I call it "heightened reality"—and become like the chameleon; to change the essence of a person is to change their habitual habits.

RA: Do you seek out really theatrical characters to portray? Is that the hallmark of Wendy Gorling's work?

WG: It's always different for me. Unlike many actors who say, "Oh, please make me look beautiful," I'll say, "You know, why don't we put a hump on my back?" or, " Can you give me a fat suit?" I love the fat suit. So costumers generally really like me, because I really try to find as much as I can make out of that costume, creatively.

RA: When I was watching you in *The Overcoat*, I was amazed at the pure pleasure in really playing. Is this a characteristic of Lecoq's teaching?

WG: Lecoq always talked about *jeu*, and *jouer jusqu'au bout*[41]...play right to the edge. In more traditional acting training, it's more about, "what is the goal?" and "what is the action?" The Lecoqian training is about action; you move your body or else you are dead. We can tell the goals and the stakes by the intensity of your body—it's very evident to the trained eye. And you can't have true passion if your body is not moving, unless it's in the pendulum of the stillness before the swing of the new impulse. When I decide to go back on the stage, I go to my roots, which is the Lecoqian training, which is, "Okay, here is something. What can I do? Okay, let's do it again. Now this way. Let's try another way now." My dynamics have to change; I always have to find the skeleton, the life of the character, and in the end, the intellect will be there.

RA: Are you talking about a non-intellectual approach, working from outside to inside, instead of building from the interior and intellectual life of the character?

WG: Yes, I mean the sitting down and mapping the whole thing in advance at the table. I don't believe in it. When I give my students character masks, I say to them, "Take a look at it. I want you to study the mask, and move it around and see what it gives you. What is your impulse of the first character you see?" They of course have an idea, but when they actually put it on, it all goes out the window. All of a sudden, the student is living within the mask, and the intellect of the student is trying to make decisions, and usually the first step is a clever decision.

RA: We're talking about impulse and intuition. But many young performing arts students want to work in more psychological theatre. They feel the need to understand something on an intellectual level about the scene, the play, the character. Is there a way to marry those two forces, what we call working from the outside in, versus inside out, with an analysis of the character?

WG: Yes, I think you definitely can. The only thing is, you have to do it playfully, instead of seriously with great ego, because you can be quite marvellous at doing the background history, but if you can't incorporate it into your heart, who cares? So that's the homework, and you bring the homework to the creation. It's whether you can then flood your whole brain, so it's not just an intellectual process—you know, trying to be smart. There is imagination in creating and I certainly have my students do that. But the great actor can then glue them together, the mediocre actor cannot. Everybody is different, they have to learn the hard way how to develop their process, and I don't think that any process is full of flowers all the way. At some point down the line, in the journey of rehearsal, you hate your work. You hate yourself. You feel you truly are not an artist. You feel you should be doing something else. The students have to learn how to acknowledge that, and say, "Okay, now I'm at the watershed, now I'm at the depths of it," and then decide to continue moving. And the tools that they have developed will bring them out into more playfulness.

RA: This fundamental idea of training young artists both to think on their feet and think about where the character is in the play, and then giving them the psychological base to tap into their imagination—this marriage seems confusing.

WG: It is confusing, unless you go to a school that is more of a physical theatre school. Studio 58 is a very physical-theatre training programme; I work with the students for a year, sometimes longer. They get a lot of alignment work, strength in the body, modern dance. Some students have gone on to work in modern dance companies. They are interested in theatre as well as dance.

RA: Wayne Specht said to me that you are the most important teacher of physical theatre on the West Coast.

41 *Jouer jusqu'au bout...* Play, perform or take it to the maximum.

WG: Really? You know, I am always talking about artistry and always talking about these twenty-year-olds who are just coming into the school as naïve and foolish as I was when I went to Lecoq's school. Then there is the shock of having this cranky lady teacher who doesn't smile very much, makes these sarcastic jokes and everything, and talks about passion, and then says don't strive for mediocrity, and tells them they're boring—all that kind of thing. They're bowled over, and it's not really until halfway through that they begin to see that I am not interested in their charming personalities, and that they are not going to get one iota of warmth. I will try sometimes to be warm, but it comes across as so false. As soon as they put their imagination on the line, I'm there for them in that instant, and I will support them 100%.

The Overcoat, 2001 television production. Wendy Gorling as Joyce. (Photo: Andrée Lanthier)

RA: In *The Overcoat*, you were responsible for the training and for the fusing of ideas and movement in the choreography and for finding the initial vocabulary, were you not?

WG: Yes, but all the moments and the choreography have to come from a "real" base. What I mean by real is a soul base. We can go as large as we can go with the character, so long as we care about the character and understand the humanity. I say to all my students, "Yeah, I can teach you to be funny, but I want you to be able to turn on a dime, so that the audience is still expecting that, and then all of a sudden, it's not funny anymore. And then you grab them, because that is what life is all about. It's easy to do, if you find the heart, the care and the real vulnerability. And what I mean by vulnerability is simply the honesty in admitting that, in fact, you are not the most important person in the world. But we all strive to be, and stories and life are about status change.

RA: I'd like to talk more about your project, *The Overcoat*. Where did that idea come from?

WG: The head of the Playhouse Theatre, Glynnis Leyshon, had seen another play that we did at the Studio 58 called *Company*. She liked it and approached Morris Panych and me to create a non-verbal play. I suggested bringing in some of the students, and it became a co-production with The Playhouse.

RA: You worked with a writer to create a non-verbal play?

WG: Morris likes theatre that is beyond speaking. He likes a large, heightened reality, and he likes challenges. He said yes to the project and by chance Morris was reading Gogol and we thought, "How about that?"

RA: Can you describe working with Morris and the students? Did the writer prepare a scenario?

WG: With *The Overcoat*, we both read it. Then we went over the story and we saw that almost all the characters were men, but we had a mixed cast. So, we looked at it from a different point of view: "What if we brought in a love interest?" and "How about instead of an old tailor, we make it a sweatshop?"

We adapted the story like that—by batting the ideas back and forth. Then we picked the music and the composer and Morris brought in Shostakovich and we had our composer.

RA: What musical works did you eventually use for the production?

WG: It was Shostakovich's Concertos 1 and 2, and jazz suites, and the ballet suites.

RA: It must be an exciting process for students, because they get to immediately apply what they are doing in school in a project.

WG: Yes, you see the light go on. Directly applying the vocabulary in a professional piece is terrific for them.

RA: It was an intense working period with Morris. Was the show a big success at the Playhouse?

WG: Well, yes. Then we remounted here, and then took it to Canadian Stage in Toronto, the National Arts Centre in Ottawa, and the Manitoba Theatre Centre in Winnipeg. You know, it is amazing that it all did do so well. Think about it: a wordless adaptation, Nikolai Gogol, Shostakovich—not exactly household names for Canadian audiences. It really had terrific word-of-mouth, and yes, it was well reviewed.

RA: From your perspective, was it good to expose the student actors to the real experience of touring, the creative process, and success?

WG: Absolutely. And they were able to really commit to all of it.

RA: Following the play version of *The Overcoat*, did you have time to keep that sense of training, then analysis?

WG: The training was always there. I couldn't stop training. Especially if the training means, "let's get deeper into the work, let's find more detail." And there is that feeling that you have to clarify for a student actor, so they can take the critique with knowledge, rather than feeling mystified, feeling that the director thinks he or she is nothing more than a puppet. I always ask my students to comment on what people have done—I want them to fully witness it, so that they can decide what their opinion is. So then, as actors working in the reality of Canadian theatre, they can survive the flood of mediocre

The Visit, 1994. Wendy Gorling as Miss Muller. (Photo: David Cooper)

directors. I teach them to be self-sufficient. I say to them always, "I am not training you to be an actor, I am training you to be a theatre artist."

RA: Where do you think all your work stands in the big picture of Canadian theatre. Is it in the freaky margins? Is it a derivative art form, outside the mainstream? What do you say to young artists about their fears about making a living, surviving, and finding ways to expand and evolve the form?

WG: I could be wrong, but I think the West is much more open. I think, in fact, a lot of the playwrights here enjoy an extended reality. Certainly, the best example that I have is working with Morris. He likes large characters. Vancouver has always been very gifted with artistic directors who are curious about physical theatre. The playwrights continued that tradition, so the audience doesn't think it's derivative or marginal. They see it for what it is. So we are always able to expand the vision and scope of what "theatre" is. Vancouver is a relatively small theatre centre, so we have loyalties. Here there are very few people working in theatre; we are just a smaller family. We see each other's work, are intrigued, and are willing to continue. I've been lucky to teach for all these years at Studio 58; a lot of our "babies" are now artistic directors, such as Roy Surette, who is now artistic director of The Belfry Theatre.

Ends of the Earth, 1992. Wendy Gorling as Willie. (Photo: David Cooper)

RA: If you had a student who showed great promise as a performer, would you send them to a school such as Lecoq's school in Paris?

WG: I want to be loyal to Canada, and yet...there really is no school. My response may sound ridiculous in many ways but—and I'm struggling with my answer—I cannot say, "Go to Lecoq's school." When I went to see the compositions of the graduates I was quite concerned because of the size of the group—almost thirty-five. But I must be careful here; I have a high regard for the work we did at Lecoq's school, but I was also in the fullness of my immature, self-centred twenties. If I had come to see our presentations I might have been absolutely appalled. But I want to be generous to these young people at the beginning of their journey. I thought there were some interesting things. They needed to explore details a lot more...but that is their journey, they will understand that. What is missing, and it's very obvious, is the genius of Lecoq. He was an explorer of life and life in the theatre. He gave his comments with the magnitude of sensitivity and the knife of honesty. He taught from a place of connection to his students...and he was brutally honest. I learned that from him. That is what people say about me, too, that I'm terribly blunt. But you know, when the students leave school, they're faced with critics, and they can be more than brutally honest, so why not be faced with honesty in theatre school?

■ ■ ■

PERFORMANCE & DIRECTORIAL HISTORY OF WENDY GORLING

Performances

2001 **The Overcoat: (film)**
The Landlady

1996 **Imaginary Invalid**
Beline and Monsieur Fleurant
Arts Club Theatre

1994 **The Visit**
Miss Muller
Arts Club Theatre

1992 **Ends of the Earth**
Various roles
Arts Club Theatre

1991 **Necessary Steps**
Various roles
Arts Club Theatre

1989 **Blithe Spirit**
Mrs. Bradman
Vancouver Playhouse

1989 **7 Stories**
Various roles
Arts Club Theatre

1984 **Peter and the Wolf**
Bird
Axis Theatre and Vancouver Symphony

1977 **Ice Wolf**
Anato
Carousel Children's Theatre

1977 **Dwelling**
Old lady.
Axis Theatre

1984 **Joined Tamanhous Theatre**

1975 **Co-founded Axis Theatre**

Direction, Movement Choreography & Movement Coaching

2002 **Flop**
Movement coach
Electric Company

2001 **Edible Woman**
Mime coach.
Vancouver Playhouse

2000, 97 **The Overcoat**
Co-direction and choreography

1998 **Goldberg Variations**
Acting coach. Ballet BC

1996 **Susannah**
Movement coach
Vancouver Opera

1995 **Spirit of the West**
Movement coach

1995 **The Company**
Co-director and movement coach
Studio 58.

1992 **Scenes from a Courtroom**
Co-director and movement coach.
Studio 58

1991 **Greeks**
Movement direction
Pink Ink Theatre

1989 **Act Without Words.**
Direction and mask movement
Studio 58

1987 **Equus**
Mask and choreography
Studio 58

1982 **Beginnings**
Co-direction and mask choreography
Axis Theatre

1979 **Metamorphosis**
Mask and mime choreography
Tamanhous Theatre

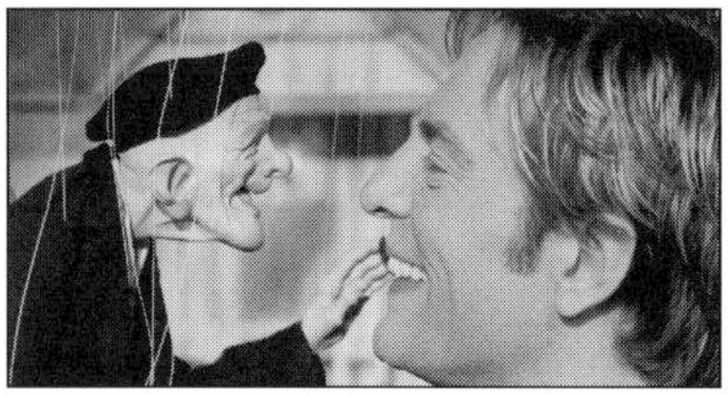

RONNIE BURKETT THEATRE OF MARIONETTES

"The biggest high for me on stage is to realize that I can control a bunch of strangers' breath, and it really is about confession, although I'm not confessing, the audience is. If I talk in a certain way, and breathe a certain way, the character is about to reveal something, until everyone stops breathing...then when the revelation is made, everybody breathes. In that little moment, the audience, unbeknownst to them, starts breathing for the puppets. I don't breathe for them; they're made of wood. They are things that get tangled and that piss me off."

RONNIE BURKETT

RONNIE BURKETT THEATRE OF MARIONETTES

The crowds lining up outside the Vancouver East Cultural Centre are clamouring to get tickets; there is an excitement, a tangible buzz of expectation. It is the kind of buzz you'd expect for a pop star or a movie star—particularly in Vancouver, where film star sightings are a common and, I'm sure, popular pastime. But, this is a line-up to see a puppet show. A puppet show for adults; no children under twelve are admitted. The adults are queuing to see *Tinka's New Dress* by Ronnie Burkett.

Tinka's New Dress is is the first of a trilogy of puppet shows all written, built, directed and designed by Burkett (with a small team of "Burkett-eers"). These works, *Tinka's New Dress, Happy,* and *Street of Blood* have catapulted him to the status of a major Canadian playwright, theatre actor, and master puppeteer.

Tinka's New Dress, 1995. Tinka. (Photo: Trudie Lee)

The key to Burkett's work, as he so eloquently puts it during our interview, is breath and focus—letting the audience breathe for the puppets. A musician would say the same about the virtuosity needed to play the cello, or any musical instrument, in fact. What Burkett does not explain is his eerie ability to disappear and reappear right before our eyes. Although he stands directly behind his puppets, in full view of the public, he can truly disappear. We become absolutely enamoured of these three-foot-tall wooden actors, and for the audience it is both astonishing and astounding. Like the pianist Glenn Gould, who had an uncanny ability to completely mesh with his instrument, Burkett has found this "magic." This is certainly part of his genius.

At its heart, *Tinka* is fundamentally very strong writing—Burkett's attention to details within details is everywhere evident as this multi-layered tale unwinds, which in the blink of an eye moves the audience from tears to side-splitting laughter. For example, during *Tinka*, Burkett creates a sideshow featuring two grotesques, Franz and Schnitzel, and then uses this podium to skewer the audience, West Coast lifestyles, the theatre, Vancouver, gay politics, himself, and even the producers of the event. The border between puppet, puppeteer and audience is broken when Burkett breaks up, laughing at his own ridiculousness. It is at this fragile moment that all the shadows and mystery the theatre provides are lifted. And it is in moments like this that Burkett shows how he can take puppetry beyond the borders, tearing down the old ideas of what can and cannot work a puppet performance.

The story of Tinka is tragic, even bleak. Why then is it such a powerful, enchanting experience? I'm convinced that Burkett,,the performer/puppeteer, allows us into his world to look for something deeper. We have a yearning to listen to stories that are compelling, and the storyteller Burkett is a masterful weaver of image and timing. With breath and focus, and the subtlest manipulation, the exquisite puppets seem alive. This is the essential magic. I believe that we transfer much of our imagination, as well as our hopes and fears and even our expectations, onto the puppets, more so than we do with live actors. His work evokes memories of childhood, perhaps even doll playing, the innocence of make-believe, sacred icons and archetypes, all at the same time.

In what seems like no time, Burkett's play has concluded. Many audience members tumble from their seats onto the stage to look very carefully at the now-lifeless puppets of Tinka, Morag, Franz and Schnitzel. The house lights are up, the moment for the theatre has passed, the story told, a multitude of silhouettes has been scorched into our memory.

I had interviewed Ronnie Burkett a few weeks earlier in Toronto where he had recently moved. His apartment, which is over a store in the Queen Street West area of Toronto, was pure Burkett: puppets, drawings, theatre posters and paintings adorn the walls. I was wondering how his move would affect his new work.

▪ ▪ ▪

RA: Ronnie, coming from Alberta, which is a very political landscape with a very small theatre scene, it must be a big move to Toronto. It's not like when you're in your twenties and you can say, "I'm going to move to the big city and take it by storm." Is there something scary about this move?

RB: It's interesting; I've been coming here for fifteen years, performing, so I know this city and I have an audience here. And, you know, the theatre community has been lovely to me. I would say that across the board. But it's weird to be forty-four years old and be the "new boy" in town.

RA: You could float into town, do your gig, and go home?

RB: Yeah. I was always from somewhere else, and when you tour like I have, for over twenty years, you are always from somewhere else, so you don't belong anywhere. So deciding to belong somewhere, I think that's been the most interesting thing for me.

RA: Your recent work has certainly created a lot of excitement. Your writing is now multi-dimensional and charged. What informs or inspires this writing?

RB: A core of longing has informed the last three shows. And when you're a gypsy, you are always longing to belong. So you get lulled into believing that you belong everywhere, and then you go everywhere. I've always realized when it was time to move on…I'm really not from here, and I'm probably going to overstay my welcome, so before they get tired of me, I will leave them.

RA: Your past has been pretty well documented, but you did start very young, and the *World Book Encyclopedia*[42] is certainly a different place to start a career.

RB: The *World Book* experience…well, it's a true story. The only thing I can say about that really is…I had no intellectual understanding about what that was all about. I looked at a passage in a book and said, "That's what I want to be." I closed the book and dreamed of being a puppeteer. I was very young, but now it makes more sense as time goes on. And certainly at this age and at this point in my life, in work and in life, I think of that story. Of course, the *World Book Encyclopedia* was an instant when I opened something up and…wham. And you know, marionette work is perfect for a loner, because you can recreate the world, and you can do it on your own. This form had no boundaries at all. I didn't know that then, but I know it more and more now.

RA: What has been the difference between creating your work in Alberta and now here in Toronto?

RB: It's interesting to be in a town where the delineations are pretty strict—you are an actor, or an actor-singer, a director,

42 When he was seven years old Burkett was looking at the *World Book Encyclopedia* and the page literally fell open to Puppetry and it was then he realized he should become a puppeteer.

or a young playwright. Even though this town has a lot of self-created artists, it still honours most "the business." I think, "Wait a minute. Just pretend you're in Alberta and nobody is telling you anything. There is no business. You just do whatever you want." This town is so rigid about theatre, and I can't get buried in it.

RA: So landscape is important. Do you think you could have developed your work outside of Alberta?

RB: No. It's funny, there was an opportunity when I was still in my twenties. I got a call while I was living in Calgary—someone called and said the Muppets[43] are doing this new series in Toronto. It was *Fraggle Rock*, which they shot for three or four years. You know I was heartbroken that I didn't get the job because I had too much experience. But had I moved to Toronto at the time, I would have been swept up into that sort of work. But I wouldn't have done the same kind of work, first of all because it's cheaper to build in Calgary, have a studio. I lived in New York in the late 1970s, for example. I kept saying that I wanted to do marionettes, but because it was the Muppet boom, everyone was saying, no one does marionettes anymore. So I didn't. While in New York, I met an old puppeteer on the street one day. He asked me, "What do you want to do?" I told him, "I really want to do marionettes." He looked me in the eye, and said, "Then get out of this city. You'll never do it here, Go home, go build marionettes." I said, "But this is the centre of the universe for puppets, and he insisted, "Go home." So I went home to Alberta and told everybody I was going to do marionette shows and they just said, "Cool!" because they didn't know what I was talking about.

RA: Were there any other puppeteers who crossed the borders, particularly from the ghetto of kids' puppets to more adult-themed works?

Happy, 2000. Ronnie Burkett and Happy. (Photo: Trudie Lee)

43 Jim Henson perfected and popularized rod-and-hand puppetry techniques when he created the Muppets for television.

Happy, 2000. Ronnie Burkett with Holocaust. (Photo: Trudie Lee)

RB: There was stuff happening in the sixties and the seventies. Felix Mirbt[44] was doing adult puppetry long before I did it. I certainly didn't start it in this country.

RA: Was it really Felix who initiated adult puppetry?

RB: I think so…he really did. You know, I saw only one of his shows, and it was late—it wasn't one of his heyday shows. But I was so aware of him and what he was doing when I was a teenager. What really struck me was that he was doing things at the National Arts Centre and at Theatre Calgary. He was doing things in real theatres, and that was stunning to me. He wasn't in a shopping mall or a school gym, and even Americans were not doing that at the time. Felix actually laid some serious groundwork.

RA: So did the work of Mirbt give you the idea that it might be possible to bring your work into the theatre?

RB: Well, another big spurt was when the Fringe Festival movement started in the early 1980s…that's something I credit for my little entrée. Up until that point I had been doing

44 Felix Mirbt's productions *Woyzeck* and *Dream Play played* at the Centaur Theatre, Canadian Stage, and the National Arts Centre, plus various European and North American tours. Mirbt's career, starting at the age of ten in his native Germany, spanned six decades and produced an extraordinary body of work. He was a master of his craft. In the words of one colleague, "He could make a pencil cry." But it was his vision and startling originality of thought that carried him on a lifelong quest to break the boundaries of conventional theatre through the use of structure, image and what he termed the "totemic object." This internationally renowned master of the art of puppetry passed away on July 15, 2002, at the age of seventy.

my work in all the "traditional" venues—in schools, malls—but when the first Fringe started in Edmonton, I was able to do my stupid little show, but then hang out with other "freaks."

RA: So the Fringe really was a launch pad for you, to make this leap from school touring to the theatre, so you could tell different kinds of stories?

RB: My only community as an artist had been puppeteers, who were all somewhere else, and that's what I thought I was. And interestingly enough, that's how I define myself now, but suddenly I thought, "Okay, I'm not the only one sitting in my little hovel thinking 'Hmm, why can't I be in a theatre somewhere? Why can't puppets do shows for adults?'" At the Fringe you see clown-based work and dance-based work. I thought, "I guess I'm not the only one thinking about knocking on that door saying, 'Let me in.'"

RA: Were you always interested in theatre?

RB: Yes, pretty much from the get-go, because of one mentor in particular, a man called Martin Stevens, whom I first encountered by letter when I was about twelve. I took his little correspondence course on puppetry—twenty sessions, you got one every week in the mail. And you know what? It is still the basis of my technique. But that subversive old man actually had sections on playwriting and vocal work. The basis of my vocal technique, which I know is pretty strong, came from that one little session in an envelope. When finally I got to meet him and stay with him he was always saying, "You're a theatre person. This is theatre. You're an actor. You're a playwright." So always in the back of my mind I was thinking, "How can I get into the theatre? What do I do?"

RA: After the puppetry-by-mail, how did you discover marionettes?

RB: I was thinking about how I could do theatrical puppetry, because there was the Muppet boom on television and they had perfected that one style of puppetry for the medium. I thought, "Well, I don't want to do that; that's not a theatrical medium. It's floppy-mouth stuff." I thought, "I'll do something that's old fashioned, that is theatrical." I loved the aesthetic of seeing the strings and I loved the control. That to me is theatrical. That's why I chose marionettes. Also it is because marionettes can't work on TV! The minute they see the marionettes working they are not watching that box. They are watching the whole package. You know, I actually had a vision of a dressing room and walking on to a stage, and the audience that was seated to watch the "play." That was so out there for me, I couldn't even tell people about it. Gosh, I told people I was gay a long time before I told them I wanted to do marionettes in the theatre. I had heard that there were actually other homosexuals, but other theatre puppeteers…none.

RA: You are pretty much self-taught, except for this mail-order puppetry course by Martin Stevens?

RB: Yeah, and I'll tell you, he was a bully. He told me, "Now go and find a singing teacher." So I studied singing. Then he said, "Now go learn to move." So when I was in New York I took two dance classes a day. I went to figure classes, for drawing. Martin was a relentless bully, and I loved him for it. I actually did go to theatre school for a year and a half…I went to Medicine Hat College for one year with Sarah Stanley, and then I went to Brigham Young University[45] and was asked to leave, then I went to New York. I guess what I did was go learn what I had to learn.

RA: Do you think you'll be able to create and work and write here in Toronto as well as you were able to in Calgary?

RB: I'll be honest. I moved here because of love, not because of career and I'll tell you, I have moments of great anxiety when I think, "Will I be able to create here?" I don't know. I had an anxiety attack yesterday while I was looking at a studio. I looked at five studios, and I've decided to take one. They left me alone for a few hours with my tape measure, and I began to visualize how I would set the studio up, and then how much to move here. I create in such a specific way; the last decade certainly has been tour, tour, tour, then go back to Calgary and see no one. My studio was quiet—none of those city sounds out there. I could just focus on creating the

45 Brigham Young University, a Mormon university based in Utah.

work, and then take it out in the world and tour. So my creative process is one of silence and stillness and calm, with no community. And it's always active in Toronto, so I'm going to have to either change or find a way to block the urban buzz.

RA: You mentioned your process, and that you work alone, in silence and calm. Where do you find your ideas and inspiration?

RB: I never know where they come from…I have too many stories I want to tell, so my problem is always focus. I have been rigidly disciplined my whole life, because nothing exists on that stage until I make it. The ideas come out of—whatever—something in the newspaper. But it usually starts with my emotional state. *Tinka* was written because I felt obliged to pay respect to war-torn Czech puppeteers. When I first read the story of the underground *Daisy*[46] shows, I wrote to every artist I knew and asked them, "If your life was in peril, would you keep doing the work you do? Would you change it, or stop?" I had thought that artists would always answer the first question in the affirmative. You know, not one artist said yes. That shocked me. Now I really had to write about these people; I had to imagine that kind of bravery. I do know what my answer would have been, quite frankly. So that was an emotional thing I needed to do. *Street of Blood*—I was really angry during that period. I was angry at Alberta, Ralph Klein and the whole Reform Party. We'd also had an attack on our quiet little building in Ramsay—our windows were sprayed with homophobic hate—and my rage about suppressing my whole life in Alberta went through the roof. That's where that idea came from. *Happy* was written on the basis that I might never get to be happy and that I might not listen to my instincts at the beginning of my mid-life crisis. I might just stay where I was comfortable. And if I didn't take that risk, what would it be like to aspire to happiness? As it turns out, I wrote it and started this move all at the same time. That trilogy is over, and it was all…sad.

RA: It was certainly a burst of creation, three major pieces in—what?—six years.

RB: Exactly. *Tinka* gave me a gift. When I read that one little paragraph in the book about Czech puppeteers, about the risks they'd taken…the biggest risk I ever took was creating a show for me. I stopped thinking about the market, about the Canada Council, about regional theatres. I thought, "What do I always want to do?" When I did *Tinka*, many people said, "You've changed your style." No. The answer was no, I'd found my style. This is what I do, I make more delicate creatures, because I look at characters as delicate, and it's a little more lyrical, and I don't need to be winking at the audience all the time, and so *Tinka* was the biggest gift. It just took me and because no one else was doing it, it took me and went: "Come here!" "Sit down!" "Focus!" And when I focussed, it was a lot quieter than it had ever been.

RA: Do you think you found what it is to be the poet?

RB: A few people have said things like that, and that's stunning to me, because when you're Puppet Boy and looking at the *World Book Encyclopedia*, and puppetry-by-mail books, then playing at the malls for too many years, you think, "I will never be a poet." I'll admit that from *Tinka* on, I became a good actor and I had to challenge myself. I started learning stuff about writing, because before that it had been writing to support the puppets I'd built, and then it switched. The puppets now support what I'm writing.

RA: Do you build first?

RB: No. Every process is different.

RA: So it's organic?

RB: It really is. *Tinka*'s script is written in palettes; every scene has a colour. I wrote it and then I started building it. Because it takes at least eight or nine months to build the show—and that is not enough time—I daydream for a year, while I'm on tour, and I write doodles. That's what I do; I've been doodling for a year now. And then there comes a time to sit down and write some rubbish that's called the first draft; that then nails the characters. My only rule is, the heads get sculpted really soon.

46 Daisy Plays, subversive puppet plays performed during the Nazi occupation of Czechoslovakia.

RA: So that picture of the characters is made "concrete" in the puppet heads?

RB: It's actually the sound, because I have a rule—if I can do the voice of the character while I'm sculpting, then it's the character. It's the visual and the aural combined. I have sculpted beautiful puppet heads that stunned me, but I couldn't do a voice for them...so I've had to trash them. So I just keep sculpting until I can sit there and talk like Edna Rural, for example, or like Happy. Then I go, "That's it!" And oftentimes, I leave the heads sitting on the worktable, for months; I don't make the molds.

RA: Do you carve from wood?

RB: The heads are carved with plasticine, and then we make moulds, castings. There are duplicates, and then they can sit for months. We start building because that's such a long process, and then I can start rewriting once I'm building the puppets. Then I start designing the bodies and carving, seeing how the leg moves. Then I sit in my wood shop in the basement, talking out loud while I am building, and then improvising, because I've got the character in my hand.

RA: Is there an immediate, concrete, physical connection to the object?

RB: What I can do, at least at the minimum, is have the heads all sculpted. I can actually write out loud. I'm improvising the scene, talking, setting the rhythm. The second draft is the most organic draft. The first is just to say I wrote a draft, which is a deadline kind of thing.

RA: It's more formalized, but it seems that what you're describing is rather like what children do with dolls, giving them a voice. It's very childlike. Do you agree?

RB: Yeah. When I created *Old Friends* for the Manitoba Theatre for Young People, it was very different. I actually just built sixteen puppets of seniors, and showed up in the rehearsal hall, and the composer Cathy Nosaty and I played, and said, I don't know who this is... *Happy* was a little different. Each process is different. It is having the character in my hand, their head in my hand literally, and being able to do the voice. I go, "Here we go, now we can begin." Let me clarify, it's the building process that is different from that point on. And even that's changed, because I've collaborated with the same people for years; there is a trust now.

RA: Have you ever tried to open up that process and allow a director to help shape what is happening on stage?

RB: Interestingly enough, I actually had worked with directors up until *Tinka*. And I realized that I was biting my tongue the whole time because I had already built it and designed the set. And I realized that those poor people were coming in and trying to make some choices and decisions, when actually it had all been decided. So as a result, when I said to myself, "I'm going to do *Tinka* for me," I was terrified of building these little delicate things, doing something that was sombre. I wanted to give myself no director. I wanted to see what I could come up with. Unfortunately, I got quite pigheaded about that little treat. For my own work, up to and including *Street of Blood*, I would write in all the stage directions.

RA: You did this for all the movements for the puppets?

RB: Absolutely. I would sit at my computer and write out: "Okay, I've just gone off stage left and I've got a puppet in my right hand. So some other puppets are entering and they should go into my left hand. I would have a logistics script. So by the time we staged *Street of Blood*, it was such a boring rehearsal, because I already knew. It was John Murrell[47] who said to me between *Street of Blood* and *Happy*, "Here's my challenge for you: write no stage directions. Just write it, and design yourself a real environment and have a real rehearsal. Don't worry about staging." I asked him, "What if I write five characters on stage?" He said, "Then write five characters on stage." So the result was that *Happy* was a glorious rehearsal process, because I figured out staging in the moment, and was able to cut the script in the moment.

RA: So the process has evolved, become more improvisational, more risk-taking?

47 John Murrell, Canadian playwright (*Memoir, Waiting for the Parade, The Faraway Nearby*), translator (*Uncle Vanya, The Seagull, Oedipus Rex*), composer, librettist, actor, director and teacher, is currently the artistic director at The Banff Centre.

RB: And a big part of the process now is "longer rehearsal." My dream would be to get the script to a skeletal position, then build all the puppets, and then have four or five months in a rehearsal hall with a composer, and just play. I am certainly not ruling out working with a director again. There are people I admire, and I'm thinking there is a way to invite them into the process. I'm not sure. I hope I can work with someone who can focus on my interpretation of text.

Street of Blood, 1998. Ronnie Burkett and Eden Urbane. (Photo: Trudie Lee)

RA: It must be very difficult to find a director who understands that so much of the impact of the puppets is conveyed by minute gestures and timing, plus your own performance. Collaboration with your team must be quite critical.

RB: My little team is so brutal with me, because I invite them to be part of this. I'll run in with some text and they'll say, "That's stupid," or "You've already said that," or "That's really funny." They are not being brutal to be cruel to me, they are just so in the process with me that they want those characters to tell the story.

RA: As you describe your process for the puppets, are you their director, their lighting designer?

RB: I have a great gift that a lot of theatre artists don't have. My playwright, my designer, my director, my producer, my actor, and my shop technician are all on stage at the same time together…all the hats are on and I'm aware of why that section worked last night for the audience. I'm constantly alert. In "real theatre," the producers, and directors and the designers all go away after opening night. So my whole team stays there for the whole rhythm of building and performance.

RA: You also have a powerful inner editor, and a strong team that surrounds your work, collaborating.

RB: Great team. Here is a funny thing. The trilogy of scripts is being published.[48] I actually spent the summer working on them, but only had the second drafts in my computer, so I had to get the stage manager's script, because she writes down every ad lib, and the rule is, if I've ad libbed it more than three times, it's in the script. Then I cut things, or they get forgotten. I forget them because I'm the writer and they're not that interesting. Some of the sequences, like Franz and Schnitzel for *Tinka*, were totally improvised every night, never written down, so I had to come up with eight years of the best of Franz and Schnitzel. It was an interesting process for me, because the shows really do grow—with the *Tinka* and *Street of Blood* tours, I took them home and recostumed the entire thing. We perhaps made some fast choices and those were wrong and I'm not happy until it's totally right. I only look at stuff from above. If I see a little glob of hot glue, the show's

48 *The Memory Dress Trilogy* was published by The Books Collective in 2002.

gone. I just say, "That's shabby workmanship." My team actually knows that hand-stitching will make it better…if then I look at it, and I think it's perfect, I can do the story. If I'm looking at what I consider shoddy workmanship, then I get cranky and miserable.

RA: So the high level of craft and presentation is essential for you.

RB: I think the biggest charm of the work is that the audience knows that I built everything. They know I give a shit, and I think that's rare. I'm not just hired to do this—I need to do this. It's artificial; it's two hours where we are all going somewhere. But it's one thing to go to listen to actors. Actors are real. What I ask people to do is go into three-foot scale, care about something that is not real, and that is phenomenal.

RA: So, it's very fragile.

RB: It's extremely fragile. It's interesting that in the last couple of years, I've been able to understand what my vocabulary is. I've been working all these years, but now I know the basis of my vocabulary, how I can manipulate people into caring about these things. It has a lot to do with the way we think about icons and how icons have been used. As an example, Mary and Jesus in three-foot scale are used to make people fearful or reverent, so people already have an association with icons. I used to think that people had no frame of reference for icons when they walked into the theatre, but they do.

RA: Is it a kind of transference?

RB: Yeah, although some people are really damaged. Some people with serious Catholic damage hate puppets; they are puppet-phobic. And that's real for them. But, really, manipulation has got nothing to do with anything other than focus and breath. I used to have this rule, up to and including the *Awful Manors* days—whatever character I was talking to, I would look at him or her. The audience will look where I am looking, and I will give this thing life. Then when Denise Clark[49] came in for a week to work with me on *Tinka*, she said, "Can't we hang him up with a string or something, then you walk away?" I said, "No!" There is a rule: you have to animate, animate, animate. You can't hang it up—the puppet dies. So we tried. We threw some fishing line over a pipe and hung the puppets up. Sure enough, if I gave them breath and focus, they were still alive; there was something really powerful happening here. So the exploration began by breaking some of the old rules. In *Tinka*, I was down there with them, playing that game, and also doing the Franz and Schnitzel improv. In *Street of Blood*, I was three feet above the puppets, which is the first time I had ever gotten out of their realm…the challenge for *Street of Blood* was monologues with puppets, because every book says you can't do that. There were three characters doing flat-out monologues right to the audience, inner dialogue. I needed to get out of their playing space and I needed to get above them. Plus I was also playing Jesus, who appears to all three of them, and I needed to be a bit higher. In *Happy*, I actually wanted to distance myself a little more. I wanted to hang a puppet and see it, then be talking with it, then walk away from it, but be on the other side of the stage looking at it, so the audience is looking at this static thing, this still-in-repose figure. That was the exploration in *Happy*. Every show does have a challenge. I'm breaking the rule, because some puppet book said that you must never do this or that…actually you can break all those rules, if you breathe and focus. The biggest high for me on stage is to realize that I can control a bunch of strangers' breath. It really is about confession, although I'm not confessing, the audience is. If I talk in a certain way, and breathe a certain way, the character is about to reveal something, until everyone stops breathing…then when the revelation is made, everybody breathes. In that little moment, the audience, unbeknownst to them, starts breathing for the puppets. I don't breathe for them; they're made of wood. They are things that get tangled and that piss me off. They are just instruments. This has less to do with me now, it's actually about them, the audience…

RA: You describe the breath and focus for puppetry; it seems closer to playing a musical instrument. Would that be an accurate comparison?

49 Denise Clark,the Calgary-based actor, choreographer and teacher, is well known for her collaborations with One Yellow Rabbit Theatre Company.

RB: Martin Stevens, my teacher and mentor, said, "Doing a puppet show is like playing the organ, because when you learn to play the organ, it's all individual elements. It's stops, pedals, and keys and flipping the sheet music, and you have to rehearse those separate elements. You have to rehearse all the separate elements, and trust me, if you rehearse and practice enough, at one point, in your pulling and pedaling and playing and flipping pages, you are no longer worried about individual elements, you are playing music. You have to rehearse until it is music." He was right; it really is about rehearsing to the point where I don't think. That's what I tell

Street of Blood, 1998. Eden Urbane. (Photo: Trudie Lee)

young theatre students; keep working. Work anything in front of an audience. I've been working 250 nights a year. Good or bad, influenza, or a cold, a bad relationship or good, I have to go on stage every night, I have to do that dance every night. You certainly learn that way.

RA: So analysis is also an important part of the process, once the show is up and running?

RB: That is the most interesting thing about this period of work in my life, because I'm actively, happily thinking about my vocabulary. I do analyze every night. That's why I'm up until five in the morning after a show, because my brain is just dissecting those moments...all those levels, producer, director, designer, actor...happily so.

RA: What about new work? Moving your studio?

RB: We're going to keep the three touring shows in Calgary. My stage manager and technician, Terry Gillis, knows how to ship them. Those three shows will get retired after 2003. We'll trash the scenery and the puppets will come to Toronto.

RA: So you do have long-range plans for the repertory?

RB: I didn't until recently, but with new pieces coming up, we can't have five shows in rep. That's just ridiculous. You know, I could perform *Tinka* forever; it's the most marketable first-date piece. I could certainly do *Happy* at a lot of venues. I do feel done with them, or that I am coming up to being done with them. I'd like to say goodbye to them all at once. These shows are also about a time in my life, a personal reflection.

RA: In the meantime, are you creating a new work?

RB: I am actively writing two shows, and I think there is a third one. Two of them are for Theatre of Marionettes, but I'm actually thinking about doing a show without puppets—Ronnie, one-man-shows without puppets. I've talked about this idea with a few people and producers from around the globe are saying, "We'll do it." I am calling it *The Likes of Me.* It's monologue-based work for five characters. Interestingly enough, they are all puppeteers. But I'm not building any puppets. It is really about five things I could have become, featuring some of the characters that I have encountered during my life. The only prop would be a puppet. I've told everybody, "I'll tell you when you can have it." People have tried to book it already but I've said no. This one will be ready when it's ready. I'm going to be the writer-in-residence at the Canadian Stage,[50] so it will afford me the time. The others will

50 The Canadian Stage Company is a large regional theatre in Toronto.

be marionette pieces; I realized that the company needed a deadline so that the team could book their lives. Building that long, costuming that long, rehearsing that long, it takes a minimum of six months for carving and jointing, so I could realistically say, it'll be ready in the fall of 2003. The trilogy I just completed was underlined by memory, sadness, grief, and the holocaust. I can keep talking about those things but I have nothing new to say. So I wondered what I want to talk about. It's beauty. I want to talk about what we do to become it, and if we can't be it, what we do to own it. And if we can't own it, what we do to destroy it.

RA: You have started to take your work across borders, to the USA and England. What does that do for your work, besides exposure?

RB: I like it. I have my regular stops in Canada, but the advantage when I perform here in Canada now is that I don't have to explain the form; we just focus on the content. When I'm touring into the States, the American audiences have no idea that I was once the "bad boy of puppetry." They don't know the form. They don't know that I stand on stage and work the puppets, so it's all very new for them. Plus there is the content. So it's thrilling to go there, although sometimes I

Happy, 2000. Carla and Drew. (Photo: Trudie Lee)

wished they had some preconceived notions and knew the form. Europe can be hard because we do festivals which tend to be shorter runs—although we did play at the Barbican in London for a month, which was heaven. This winter I'm going to Adelaide, Australia, where we'll be performing for three weeks. I still like it; I have found a life that I want to stick around, but I have built a career on touring; I have to reconcile myself to that.

RA: What do audiences in Europe, which has a long history of marionette and puppetry, think of your work?

RB: This is the most shocking thing I've learned about my place in puppetry. I had assumed there were other artists in pockets, or puppeteers in certain cultures who were doing new text-based work in theatres. But it is very rare. What makes me a freak is that I do text-based work, and that I am the playwright. In my own country, I'm seen as a playwright, and in my own country I've been acknowledged as an actor. That has sent shock waves around the puppet world. I've realized that they are all stuck in the European mould; for them, puppetry is basically a visual and movement form, and no one has been encouraged to write. Now we have the "puppet-Nazis," the puppet theorists, centred at the institute in Charleville-Meziers,[51] France, which is run by Roman Paska. He is the new director and has declared: "Puppets should not talk. They don't work when they talk."

RA: More puppet rules?

RB: Yeah, by a cutting-edge contemporary guy. I did argue with him over a glass of wine, but he has stayed so distant from me, although he has at least come to see my work. At a recent Henson Puppet Festival in New York, they had a symposium on "puppets and the voice" and they agreed that puppets shouldn't talk…ever. I hear the wind whistling around me. So, in fact during the last year, I've decided to write essays, and I've had some encouragement from old-time puppeteers to challenge Roman Paska and others, naming their names and saying they are wrong. I think I know why they make those broad statements. It's because they aren't trained as vocal actors. They don't know how to interpret text, so they teach what they know. In fact, for me it is really lonely out there. But what is really interesting is that everywhere I go, I meet the twenty- to thirty-year-old puppeteers who have been trained at the institute in Charleville-Meziers by Roman Paska, or at the O'Neill Institute at the University of Connecticut, both hallowed places to learn about puppetry. These kids are coming up to me and saying, "I've written a play, but I can't show it to you. What do I do with it now?" So I feel that it is critical that we teach these young puppeteers how to act vocally. Let's say, "Fuck the puppet for a minute; let's work on the text. And then let's marry them." I would love that kind of thing to start happening.

RA: Do you have a protegé? Are you mentoring anyone?

RB: No, I didn't think that way until the twenty-year-old puppeteers started contacting me. I said no, because all they want to learn is Muppets. I thought my mentoring would be teaching people how to make marionettes, and then I realized that's not what I wanted to teach.

RA: Teaching the actual construction and preparation?

RB: No, they can learn that elsewhere; they should learn that on their own. The only way to learn building techniques is to learn how to fail miserably.

RA: Where would you suggest that a twenty-year-old with a passion for puppetry go for training?

RB: That's a hard question, because of the skills base…

RA: Is there anything in Canada?

RB: No. By necessity they have to learn how to build things, which takes up most of the curriculum. Then they have to perform, which is usually stuck to one style of performance, because they are following a teacher. For instance, Bart Roccoberton, at the University of Connecticut, does it pretty much on his own. How Bart does it, I don't know. He turns out phenomenal students. He is a man of many talents; he doesn't have the luxury of theatre departments. What I'm

51 Institut international de la marionnette, marionette and puppetry school based in Charleville-Meziers in northern France.

interested in is either students who are constantly learning all the disciplines, or who just say, I am a designer of puppets. Not a performer. You know, for almost ten years Luman Coad[52] and I have been talking about founding a National Puppet School of Canada. He is ready to do it, but neither of us has the willpower to find the funding. It would be a conservatory program, and we know each other's strengths and weaknesses. I think I am a good ambassador for puppetry, although I don't know if I would be the best person to set up a curriculum.

RA: A curriculum about breaking the rules and creating new forms?

RB: Yeah, it would be amazing to put sixteen to twenty brilliant know-it-alls in one place, and watch them duke it out. They should have the experience of trying it all.

RA: Any other advice for the next generation?

RB: Yeah. Become an actor would be my advice. You can always learn how to make *papier mâché*. You can always find someone to build something. Surround yourself with actors and writers—the real theatre. Start in the real theatre. Build your community from that place. That's my advice. And do it in a place where you can afford to do it. And if you are that keen, you can build puppets on the side. Learn to breathe and use the voice, then find out about puppets.

RA: From your experience of being self-taught, do you know now what an artist in your field needs to succeed, to make his or her mark? And can that be taught?

RB: One of the things that I need, and the thing that has been best for me because of necessity, of economics—is the constant act of repetition. I've only become an artist because I've had to repeat over and over and over. I see that what is really lacking for theatre artists is time to create, then understand the work. I am lucky because I have to repeat these shows several hundred times.

■ ■ ■

Happy, 2000. Cleo. (Photo: Trudie Lee)

52 Luman Coad, puppeteer and director of Coad Canada Puppets, based in Vancouver.

EXCERPT FROM STREET OF BLOOD*

RONNIE BURKETT THEATRE OF MARIONETTES

EDNA: I've been awake all night. Two Neo Citrans and I still couldn't sleep. Maybe it was the late show that did it. They were showing that old Esmé Massengill movie, Passport to Love. It was one of my favourites. Esmé played Dixie Carlyle, a waitress in a roadside diner who changes a flat tire for a travelling foreign prince and falls in love. Oh, so romantic. But that was our Esmé. Living, breathing passion.

Light dims somewhat CS. Ronnie leaves Edna sitting in her chair and crosses to the SL bridge tower, walking Young Esmé #3 onto the catwalk. This is a contained pool of light, revealing Esmé in a spectacular white satin wedding dress with a pale pink beaded veil. Again, Esmé stands alone and the people to whom she is speaking are unseen. This is heavily underscored with movie music.

ESMÉ/DIXIE: Oh Betty, oh Audrey, oh Delores, you're the best friends a gal could ever have. Thanks for coming to a foreign country just to be my bridesmaids. I'll miss you all and the happy times we had at the diner. Oh sure, here they'll call me Princess, but I'll always be Diner Dixie to you. Please know that I will never forget you, nor will I ever forget that it was slinging hash that brought me to the palace gates. But now I say goodbye, my beloved Ladies in Waitressing, for my heart has a new destination and my passport is love!

She turns upstage as the music swells. SFX of honking car horn and screeching tires as SL light to black. Young Esmé is hung backstage, Ronnie crosses to CS bridge and Edna's light restores.

EDNA: Too bad poor Dixie Carlyle tripped on her train and got hit by a speeding taxi as she crossed the street to the church. But she died beautifully, and oh, I loved that dress! More than anything I had ever seen. So when my Stanley asked me to help run the farm—which was his idea of a marriage proposal—I just knew that my wedding dress had to be like the one in *Passport to Love.*

I saw that movie three times down at the old Bijoux, trying to doodle the dress in the dark. I clipped every picture I could find of it from the movie magazines. I worked extra hours at Turner's Drugstore during the week, just so I could save enough money to buy five yards of satin and two of lace from the catalogue. I made my pattern from old newspapers, then I cut it out of sugar sacks, just like I use for my quilting, as a kind of test run. Then I scrubbed down the kitchen table, laid out my precious cloth, and cut. Lord love a duck, I had never been so nervous in my whole life. It took me weeks to sew that dress, because I knew that fancy clothes in France were all hand sewn. And since necessity is the mother of invention, I stained the lace veil pink by dipping it in a bucket of diluted saskatoons I'd put through the sieve.

Leaving Edna seated in her chair CS, Ronnie crosses to SL bridge.

I knew I was no Esmé Massengill, and even though I stopped eating the week before the wedding, I was still just lumpy Edna. But when I put on that dress, well, didn't I just feel like a princess.

Young Edna #1 enters through the alley between the SL and CS bridges. She is in her wedding dress, a copy of the one from Esmé's movie. She walks SLC to a phrase of "Here Comes The Bride," and is hung in position there.

It was a small wedding and I had only one gal stand up with me, not a tribe of bridesmaids like Esmé. There was no money for that, and besides, I didn't have that many friends.

Light up on Cora Jean at the SL bandstand.

But Cora Jean Pickles, who worked with me at the drugstore, agreed to be my bridesmaid and matron of honour combined. Cora Jean was saving up her money to go to Winnipeg to study the ballet. It was Cora Jean who gave me the beads for my veil. Took them right off one of her dance recital dresses. I was indebted to her for life because of that.

Light fades out on Cora. Ronnie crosses back to the CS bridge and Edna.

I don't remember much about my wedding day. Oh, I know it's supposed to be the most important day in a woman's life, but I had worked and worried so much on an empty stomach that I was in kind of a fog. Mind you, the fog lifted that night when Stanley took his husbandly right with me. Suddenly I didn't feel like a princess anymore. The next morning I wrapped that dress in tissue paper and put it away in the cedar chest.

Light SL dims on young Edna, but not to black.

We got on with our married life, which was surprisingly not much different from life before. I grew to tolerate Stanley climbing on top of me at night, sometimes imagining that he was Armand Collier or Trevor St. Clair or some other movie star lover. Looking back I realize now that it never really took that long, although it seemed like an eternity at the time. But it was my duty, and it would hopefully lead to something.

But it never did. After awhile, I went to old Doctor Beaton to see if I was doing something wrong. But no, he assured me that we were doing everything right. It was my body that was wrong. It could not and would not make a baby. They used to call it barren. Like the prairie when the fields are empty. That was me. Empty, through and through.

When I got home, Stanley was still out doing chores. To this day I don't know why, but I went to the cedar chest, took out my wedding dress and put it on. And went upstairs and sat on the bed. It was the only night in my married life when I didn't make supper.

Light up, just barely, on young Edna SL. SM hands Ronnie a black cap, which he puts on as Stanley.

Stanley found me sitting there. He didn't say a word. Not a peep. Stood in the doorway staring at me. I couldn't look at him, but I told him. "I can't have a baby" was all I said. Stanley was so quiet. He left the room. I stayed on the bed, memorizing the rag rug on the floor, listening to him downstairs. An awful noise. I thought he was breaking things, or packing to leave. I didn't know.

Light intensity shifts somewhat in a subtle cross fade from Edna in chair CS to young Edna SL. CS does not fade to black. Continuing Edna's storytelling, Ronnie leaves the CS marionette, walks toward SL and climbs off the bridge to deck level. He is Stanley. During the following monologue, Ronnie enacts what Edna is describing. The bacon and eggs are mimed, but the apron is real, and he ties it onto the marionette during the description.

And then he was there again. He set something down on the bureau, walked over to me and tied an apron around me while I sat. Then he took what he had set on the bureau and put it on my lap. I looked down and there was a plate. Bacon and eggs. He knelt down, took a piece of bacon in his fingers, and held it up to my mouth. That's when we looked at each other. We stayed there for a long, long time. Me in my wedding dress and an apron, Stanley on his knees before me. Me and my man. Mr. and Mrs. Stanley Rural. Crying over a plate of bacon and eggs.

He ends on his knees, embracing young Edna. The tableau of Ronnie and young Edna in her wedding dress is held as the SL light fades very slowly to black.

■ ■ ■

Street of Blood, 1998. Mrs. Edna Rural and Dolly. (Photo: Trudie Lee)

* Excerpt reprinted with the permission of the author.

PRODUCTION HISTORY OF
RONNIE BURKETT THEATRE OF MARIONETTES

2002 **Provenance**
In production. Co-produced by Wiener Festwochen, Vienna, The Barbican Centre, London, queerupnorth, Manchester, and Canadian Stage Company, Toronto. Slated to premiere at Theatre Network, Edmonton, November 2003, with domestic and international touring booked throughout 2004.

2002 **Billy Twinkle (working title)**
In development.

2000 **Happy**
Premiered at duMaurier World Stage, Toronto. Co-produced with World Stage, Harbourfront Centre, Theaterformen 2000 and The Barbican Centre. Subsequent runs: Usine C, Montreal, Theaterformen 2000, Braunschweig, The Barbican Centre, London, Theatre Network, Edmonton, One Yellow Rabbit and Alberta Theatre Projects, Calgary, Manitoba Theatre Centre, Winnipeg, Canadian Stage Company, Toronto. Production still touring, with spring 2003 tour to the United Kingdom.

1998-02 **Street of Blood**
Premiered at Manitoba Theatre Centre, Winnipeg. Subsequent runs: National Arts Centre, Ottawa, Theatre Network, Edmonton, One Yellow Rabbit, Calgary, Canadian Stage Company, Toronto, Henson International Festival of Puppetry and New York Theater Workshop, New York City, queerupnorth, Manchester, Sodra Teatern, Stockholm, The Brighton Festival, England. Production retired June 2002 at The Tramway, Glasgow, Scotland.

1996-98 **Old Friends**
Co-produced with and premiered by Manitoba Theatre For Young People, Winnipeg. Subsequent runs: The Calgary International Children's Festival, The Milk Festival, Toronto, Saskatoon Children's Festival, Regina Children's Festival, La Maison Theatre, Montreal, Young People's Theatre, Toronto.

1994-02 **Tinka's New Dress**
Premiered at Manitoba Theatre Centre, Winnipeg. Subsequent runs: Canadian Stage Company, Toronto, Festival de Theatre des Ameriques, Montreal, Usine C, Montreal, National Arts Centre, Ottawa, One Yellow Rabbit, Calgary, Theatre Network, Edmonton, Vancouver East Cultural Centre, Vancouver, Henson International Festival of Puppetry, New York City, Dublin Theatre Festival, Ireland, Images Festival, Holland, Theatreformen 2000, Hannover, Theatre Bellevue, Amsterdam, queerupnorth, Manchester, The Barbican Centre, London. Production retired in October 2002 at The Melbourne Festival, Australia.

1993-94 **The Daisy Theatre**
At The Secret Theatre (One Yellow Rabbit), Calgary.

1991-93 **Awful Manors**
Premiered at Theatre Network, Edmonton. Subsequent runs: Canadian Stage Company, Toronto, National Arts Centre, Ottawa, Manitoba Theatre Centre, Winnipeg, Alberta Theatre Projects, Calgary.

1989-90 **The Punch Club**
Premiered at Nexus Theatre, Edmonton. Subsequent runs: Lunchbox Theatre, Calgary, Manitoba Theatre Centre, Winnipeg, Factory Theatre, Toronto, Station Street Arts Centre, Vancouver.

1988 **Virtue Falls**
Premieresd at Lunchbox Theatre, Calgary. Also played at Nexus Theatre, Edmonton.

1986-88 **Fool's Edge**
Premiered at Alberta Theatre Projects. Subsequent runs: The Edmonton Fringe Festival, Workshop West Theatre, Edmonton, One Yellow Rabbit, Calgary, Winnipeg Fringe Festival, du Maurier World Stage, Toronto, Factory Theatre, Toronto.

JEST IN TIME THEATRE

"The thing about Jest in Time is that we are a creation company. We are a group of people who have made the commitment to work together, which is really hard to do. Over the fifteen or eighteen years we've worked together, we've had this argument back and forth about the process. It's hard to find people who will actually commit to that much work, that much time together. So the process sort of grows over time. We are still kind of an oddity in Canadian theatre because we have worked exclusively just the four of us since 1986."

—CHRISTIAN MURRAY, JEST IN TIME

Quirky Quartet

Based in Halifax, Jest in Time is an energetic quartet of mime/actors, Sherry Lee Hunter, Christian Murray, Shelley Wallace, and Mary Ellen MacLean. Their work is consistently innovative, and over the past fifteen years or so they have created a substantial body of work. The company is the brainchild of Sherry Lee Hunter, who had early inspiration at the Canadian Mime Theatre School in Niagara-on-the Lake. Sherry Lee went on to further her training with Leonard Pitt, the California-based teacher, and then she discovered the teacher and mentor, Tony Montanaro, in Maine. She returned to Canada and began teaching theatre classes. It was through her teaching that she met up with fellow Maritimers Mary Ellen MacLean and Christian Murray. In 1986, the American actor Shelley Wallace joined the company, and well, the rest is history.

Jest in Time is one of the last of the troupes whose founding artists are still operating the company, continuing to create new work, writing the blizzard of grant applications, producing their own shows, organizing tours. Jest in Time is a testimony to the power of a shared vision, and to the power of a quartet. They've discovered the "music" of working in a tightly knit ensemble—producing provocative, subversively funny collections of sketch comedies—and have toured to just about everywhere in Canada.

Starting a theatre company in this country, particularly in the 1980s, with the economic downturn and government cuts to just about everything, was an act of courage or madness. It was doubly courageous to start a theatre company in the Maritimes, and a physical theatre company to boot.

Evolution, 2000. L-R: Mary Ellen MacLean, Sherry Lee Hunter, Shelley Wallace, Christian Murray. (Photo: Carol Kennedy)

Jest in Time has impressive international touring credentials, and has built sharply defined work that pushes the edge of physical theatre, while still keeping a keen eye on the essential comic moment. It has also maintained a strong commitment to a creation process under the tutelage of Tony Montanaro—an American actor who studied with the great French master teacher, Étienne Decroux.

Jest in Time has also created various television specials for CBC and it continues to build its repertoire of character-driven and movement-driven pieces. Its latest original production, *Trip*, is a pointed and funny collection of sketches. They are working on it with the Halifax-based filmmaker Janet Hawkins, who created a dazzling, ever-changing video image backdrop to the troupe's new work. It is a risk for the company, for instead of looking around them for material to satirize and parody, they have turned the camera, so to speak, on themselves.

In *Trip*, there are startling juxtapositions of video images with "live scenes" of the troupe's real—and not-so-real—moments of hilarity, despair and road weariness. For anyone who has ever thought about touring in a van across this country with a group of actors for any period of time, it is a revelation. The movement is relentless and the physicality of moving together sometimes borders on poetic. The exploration of the internal moods combined with the troupe's dealing with the external world results in a fascinating meditation. As on any family road trip, family-fatigue, over-familiarity and disgust trigger hilarious fight scenes that scratch close to the truth.

What is left after *Trip*? Imagery of yellow-line fever, memories of the worst coffee in the world, a physical memory in the muscles of loading and unloading the company van, not knowing what town or time zone you are really in, and a feeling of being "out of time," in the twilight zone where time vanishes into the hum of the wheels.

There is a deeper and stronger undercurrent in this work, and it is the story about "group," how to maintain, survive and nurture a group, and it artfully reveals the paradox of taking theatre work on tour. No matter what success, excitement or applause the thousands of road and airline miles may bring in terms of endorsement, there is a yearning for home, wherever that may be.

Jest in Time is also very active in the Halifax theatre community, teaching workshops in physical comedy, improvisation, movement and mask building. The company has a studio space, but is looking to expand its local possibilities while trying to reduce the need to tour. A collective dream is to have a theatre space, as an alternative to other spaces. And on the subject of space, I will take the liberty of revealing that Sherry Lee Hunter's dream is also to be the first theatre company in space. And with this dynamic quartet, who deeply understand what it is to be four to the power of four, anything could happen.

And now for a disclaimer. All of the other interviews for this book were carried out face to face, following an initial phone interview. Unfortunately, due to blizzard conditions in both Montreal and Halifax and limited time on my part, my trip to the east coast had to be cancelled. Thus, this interview was recorded on the telephone, the only one I was not able to do in person. The telephone conversation is a four-on-one, but I must say that the Jest in Time troupe handled the interview very well. Their voices quickly became familiar, and rarely, if ever, did they step on each other's lines. That is the sign of a well-tuned company. We had a lively conversation, laced with some good Maritime-isms, which ranged from the beginnings of the company, to process, to how they are able to maintain a career and a company based in Halifax, Nova Scotia. For reading clarity, the names of the company are: Sherry Lee Hunter, SLH; Mary Ellen MacLean, MEM; Christian Murray, CH; and Shelley Wallace, SW.

■ ■ ■

RA: I'd like to begin by asking how you got together. Where did it all begin?

MEM: We got together in 1983, with Sherry Lee and Christian and me.

RA: Were you all Haligonians who hung out together?

SLH: Well. How this company came together was that I studied at the Canadian Mime School in Niagara-on-the-Lake.

RA: Oh, you did? In the late seventies?

SLH: Way back when. And then I also studied at Leonard Pitt's School of Mime in California. After that I came back to Halifax and I hung around, not so much with actors, but with dancers. It seemed all my connections were in the dance community. Then I started teaching preliminary workshops in mime and that's when I met Mary Ellen and Christian.

RA: I see, through the dance scene?

Accidental Blood, 1996. Shelley Wallace, Mary Ellen Maclean, Sherry Lee Hunter. (Photo: Cylla von Tiedemann)

SLH: Yeah, although I didn't meet them through the dance scene; I met them in 1982 because I offered an introductory mime workshop for actors and dancers, and Mary Ellen and Christian took the workshop. I have always had this vision of having a physical theatre company that could travel and tour, and do original mime plays all over the world. That was my vision. Then I asked Mary Ellen and Christian if they wanted to join this vision and they said yes; they were both in high school at that time. But really, the company began in earnest in 1986 when Shelley Wallace joined. I had gone to SUNY Purchase to study with Bob Berky, Michael Mosher and Fred Garbo.[53] While I was studying with them I met a young man named Peter Ford; he said I had to go and to meet this "Salvador Dali of Mime," Tony Montanaro. I told Mary Ellen and Christian that we had to go meet this master mime. So the three of us went down to Portland, Maine. At the time, Shelley was actually a member of Tony Montanaro's company. We have made it a point to continue studying with Tony and go down to Portland, Maine and work with him at least once a year. I would say that Tony Montanaro is the major influence on our work.

RA: Tony studied with Étienne Decroux in Paris. Would you say that the roots of your inspiration can be traced to the French master teachers?

SLH: Yeah. At the time we met Shelley, Celebration Mime Theatre was, for whatever reason, disbanding. We asked her to join our company and you know, Robert, I really believe that Jest in Time, as a company, began in totality when Shelley joined.

RA: It was, in a sense, a merger?

SLH: Well, actually, what was really good was that the type of physical theatre that we were doing was very much the same as what Celebration was doing. It was doing really universal themes and observations of life in a very abstract and funny way, using the body to create the images. I like to describe them as physical graphics. To make a long story short, our humour was the same, as were our ways of working and our goals. We instantly hit it off. And it was, I think for me, one of

53 American clowns Bob Berky, theatrical clown; Michael Mosher, contact juggler; and Fred Garbo, physical theatre comedian and director of The Inflatable Theater.

the reasons why I moved up to Halifax; it had been good to work under my master, and I was his apprentice for eight years. But then it was kind of nice to work with my peers and take what I'd learned and go out and do it.

RA: There are some questions about what physical theatre actually is. How does your company define it or redefine it?

CM: We sort of go back and forth in terms of where our company focusses, what we define as physical theatre. Sometimes we do straight-ahead verbal work and text-based work and sometimes more physical. But then, we're doing complete pantomime works, because we are so good at it at this point and no one else is really doing it. And you know, it still kind of blows people away, especially since we are not sort of doing the "mime-schmime," the classic white-face mime of Marcel Marceau. We are, however, going back to that tradition, and the tradition that comes from Tony Montanaro and his sensibility and his definition of mime, which is physical eloquence and that's kind of where we're at, you know. That's our platform, our launching pad for what we are doing. We basically take elements of mask, puppetry, slapstick, text, even stand-up comedy, and monologue work. It's been interesting to be part of that exploration and we have tried buffoon clown shows. What tends to happen is that if we cannot afford the set, then we do a mime show!

SW: Another constant stimulator for us is that we work with not just the four creators. We invite other creators as well. We recently did a show called *Love Bytes*, and we contracted different writers to write sketches for us. It was interesting because the writers knew us.

RA: By your description of finding inspiration, you are obviously not afraid to take on text-based writing or major writers and include that in your work.

SW: It's very true. We recently went out West to take part in a Samuel Beckett Festival. The performance we did was called *Play*, and it's verbal. Three characters are stuck in urns. You can't go fast enough, it says in the script. So believe it or not, that was one of the most physical pieces we've done, because of the fact of being stuck in an urn and just using your voice. It's great to push yourself in all different directions. I think that's really helped us.

MEM: I think it's whatever we need. It's taking an idea and really going at it. And whatever we need to execute that idea, we'll use. And this new play *Trip* was, first of all, a bit of a departure in that we wanted to write a play as opposed to a sketch comedy format show that is such a tradition with that kind of clowning background. We wanted to incorporate a multi-media layer and really interact with that video screen. So that took us in a whole other direction and also it's very contemporary due to the technology. So again, that's how we can use our skills as physical actors and convey this idea of a play and portray the journey through fifteen years of being on the road.

RA: What is your process for creation and how do you do this?

SLH: I've said from the beginning I didn't want to be a "dictator" artistic director. I wanted all of us to contribute and as the years go on, sometimes it works better to have a dictator and sometimes it doesn't. It goes both ways. The one thing about our group is that we all contribute equally to the creation. Everything that we create is built on the floor, up on our feet, because we have this process. And because we know each other so well, you could give us any subject right now and we could go into a studio and come out with four sketches about each idea.

RA: Do you want to talk a little bit more about that process?

CM: The thing about Jest in Time is that we are a creation company. We are a group of people who have made the commitment to work together, which is really hard to do. Over the fifteen or eighteen years we've worked together, we've had this argument back and forth about the process. It's hard to find people who will actually commit to that much work, that much time together. So the process sort of grows over time. We are still kind of an oddity in Canadian theatre because we have worked exclusively just the four of us since 1986. We've been this core creation company and our ways of creating have developed out of Tony Montenero's style of "round improvisation."

SW: Tony Montanaro lays it out really well in his books. He has created this whole idea of rounds. Our motto is that we take whatever we need to express an idea. The same thing with writing; for example, I come in with an idea. Everybody is giving 100% to that idea, but they are also helping me commit to that germ of an idea. It is like having four directors at the same time, and I'll tell you, sometimes that's like riding a wild horse. Like any ride, you just have to be careful. So, we use whatever we can. For instance, *Trip*, the sketch piece we do about a monkey family, is based on a documentary performance style. I came in to the rehearsal with that idea, and slowly we worked it through, working up on our feet. Then Christian was inspired by what he saw in the improv, went away and started writing text. Everybody brings his or her expertise into the process, so it does become collaborative. Tony's process is really good for maintaining and nurturing the group; it's never just one person's idea. I might have thought of monkeys, but it's way beyond that now. It just goes into the big stewpot of ideas, and it keeps the material organic and very fresh.

CM: We kind of distill the idea down.

SW: That's very important.

CM: We try and get to the essential. If it's a piece that we like, that we're happy with, it tends to work for the audience. We've reached that point in terms of our craft; we finally know how to make a show now. How many shows?

SW: I agree with that completely. If it cracks him up, if it cracks up Mary Ellen and Sherry Lee, then I know it's going to work. If they stand there blank-faced and go uh huh, then…

SLH: You go mad.

SW: Then we all go mad!

RA: Obviously, with a long-term relationship, you've had lots of laughs but also lots of creative differences to get that honest distillation process, which in fact is an editing process, isn't it?

SW: Well, the one thing Tony always said was, "Hey, come on, you guys. The group must just keep thinking. It's the best idea. The idea that comes the closest to defining whatever you're going for, that's the one you guys have to go after." You've got to give up your own ideas sometimes and sometimes it's hard, but it is for the big picture.

SLH: I think it's important for groups starting out to have different personality types and different people. You have to really, and I mean really, learn how to listen to each other. And if someone is a little softer—if they are not, you know, this sort of brazen type, aggressive type—you're going to have to nurture them a bit and find out what their idea is. What they are sitting on. And the aggressive types who get right out there have to be tempered, too. It's all about listening in every form and at every level possible.

MEM: And depending on the day, one is more aggressive than the other.

RA: For groups as tight as yours, does it actually get easier to create or is it a harder process to keep that open listening process?

SLH: I think it's definitely become easier. We used to go to workshops and they'd say, "Who the hell is up there in that studio fighting?" And we'd come down and have lunch together, all happy, hugging and kissing. Then we'd go back up. It's just that we're passionate. We are a passionate group. So over the years, it has definitely become easier because we don't have the energy to fight as we used to. It's not so much that we are fighting; it's just that when you put four passionate egos in the room, that's going to happen.

CM: It's hard sometimes when you don't feel you have personal autonomy over an idea. Some days it's very difficult. You say to yourself: "I want it to work and now I have to go to through the filter of three other minds." Some days it doesn't matter.

RA: Especially so, I think, when you're actually working with text. Then it's a whole other mindset. Words can be demons.

MEM: I also think that as the company matures—every time we create a new show—the stakes are higher because we have achieved a certain level and we always want to match that level or go beyond it. We want to grow as artists and grow as a company.

RA: Are you all wearing the hat of the actor, director and designer? Are you all considered equal? Or did you over the years say, "Actually, I can write"? Those levels of passions and expertise follow different directions. Has that actually evolved?

MEM: I think certainly people's strengths have evolved, but when we are in the studio, we're all writing, all creating. We all step out and we all become directors at some point. Because of the nature of being so physical and majestic, you have to have someone look at it. It's a constant co-directing.

RA: Is it tough to find a director who understands your vocabulary?

MEM: Yeah. And also over the years we've had very good collaboration with people like Bryden MacDonald, who is a Canadian playwright. I think when we benefit is when we're in the studio and we're creating. We improvise.

SLH: A very important tool now is video. That's what we've used basically our whole career. When we've worked on a subject—whatever it might be—we'd video it. Then we'd sit and look at it to see what was working and what wasn't, because unlike dancers, we don't perform in front of mirrors. So you either have one person constantly jumping in and out or you hire an outside director. And of course, you can't deny the power of the video. You can see what you are doing and compare it with what you thought you were doing. And they may be two different things.

RA: Another question about the process, about the nuts and bolts: how long do you generally take to create your work and then how do you afford whatever time you build into your creation process?

CM: Well. It's different for every piece we do. In the past we've been able to spend longer periods of time on smaller pieces. For instance, there's one piece of ours called *Handmade*, a seven- or eight-minute piece which is a very technical and complete ensemble. It is what we consider our master work—we developed it with Tony over a two-week period. Then we rehearsed the music with the sound composer, Sandy Morrow, over two months. That was over ten years ago. Our latest show *Trip* was written in six weeks.

RA: Is this actual time-up-on-your-feet writing and creation time?

CM: Five to six weeks—that was intense. Because we have worked so much together, we have a head start, so the time required changes. It depends on how technical the work is. If we're doing more "clownesque" work, we need a tiny bit less time compared to the real ensemble choreography. It just depends on the intensity of the work. And then we've done straight-ahead plays like a Sam Shepard play at Neptune Theatre, where you get three weeks rehearsal—you know the Canadian theatre rule.

Handmade, 1991. Sherry Lee Hunter. (Photo: Cylla von Tiedemann)

RA: Was this a commission or a co-production?

CM: When Linda Moore was the artistic director at Neptune, she loved our work and she actually directed *Trip*. She was the first one in this community to say, "Check these people out." She brought us in and we did some kids' shows. Then we did the Beckett with her and then we did Sam Shepard's

Sleep Tracks, 2001. Front: Christian Murray. Back, top to bottom: Sherry Lee Hunter, Mary Ellen MacLean and Shelley Wallace. (Photo: Cylla von Tiedemann)

Seduced. She really loves Sam Shepard and she really thought this particular piece would work.

RA: Was Linda inspired by the way you work as a team?

SLH: I think the reason she wanted us to do Beckett was because Beckett loved silent films. Beckett loved Buster Keaton and we were able to bring Beckett to life because of our background. It was much more refreshing in a kind of physical way than the average actor would have done.

RA: What do you have to say as a group of artists? What drives you to the rehearsal hall? What's the essential thing that drives you and drives your work?

SW: People have said, "How can you guys still be together after all these years?" It is certainly not the money. Well, the glue that keeps us together is that we love performing. We totally love the art form and the innovation of the art form. It's under our skin. There's no better high than being on stage when it really works and you know that you've created that from scratch. And we love the audience's response. There's nothing better in the world than that.

RA: Have you discovered over time the sense of "voice," what you want to say as artists, or is it that you want to keep open and eclectic? Have you found a certain style, a way of speaking or a certain voice to talk about who you are and where you are now or a specific theme that you have followed, or is it really eclectic?

MEM: I think it is eclectic because of what we are interested in. For example, in our show *Trip* we were interested in telling a story about our lives on the road. One sketch that we did was about a dysfunctional family, so we investigated that kind of relationship. But I think, overall, we have to appeal to a large audience. When we went to Japan recently, we were reminded how the work can reach such a broad audience.

CM: We don't necessarily have a political agenda that some theatre companies have that they can go back to. I think we've been excited by Tony. He is a true person of the theatre. He has been a real teacher, a fabulous teacher throughout his whole life. I think he is in his seventies now, but he still has that excitement. One of the mantras he's given us is, "Don't just write; develop the art form." And that's the thing we've been trying to do. In a way, we just keep developing wherever the wind blows us.

RA: So you tap into certain emotional moments?

CM: We don't dismiss politics. It comes in when it's right for us. But it just has to be organic, and that's just the potentiality of a physical theatre and mime.

SW: It's kind of the crazy and eclectic way we see the world: The World According to Jest in Time. I think that as an art form it's more like painting, or more like music. It is theatre, but it really has the idea of communicating more than just story. It's multi-layered—movement, story, light, physical comedy—and that's what I think excites the four of us. We have a certain style and we interpret everything through that. We have a real chemistry and that informs everything we do.

RA: Now, what about the choice to remain and work in the Maritimes?

SLH: Being here certainly influences our choices.

MEM: Partially. And again, our voice. Our voice comes from where we are. We live here. We don't live in Alberta. We don't live in metro Toronto. We live in Halifax, in this particular region, and we've been together for eighteen years.

MEM: Exactly. We are not viewed as freaky alternative because we are, as I've said, "accessible." But we are certainly pushing the boundaries of what theatre can be.

CM: I think sometimes we do feel a tiny bit ignored down here for the type of work we've been doing. But that's just because we are so isolated and it's hard to get your work out there without having to take huge, huge financial risks. To just keep a theatre of any sort going, especially one that is actually artistic rather than dinner theatre or commercial theatre. Theatre is expensive. We've had interesting and varied experiences between touring theatre—we've been all over the world—and doing television specials. We've done three television specials with CBC.

RA: Have you ever been tempted to make a lot of money doing the symphony show—developing characters set to music and then just going to large venues with symphony orchestras? Or have you always taken your own temperature and decided, "No. The creative process is really about us."

MEM: Well, actually, we are working on a symphony show this week. And last year we did also some work with the symphony. So that's something that we are definitely interested in doing. And we have been pursuing it in the last few years because it is a great thing to have.

SW: But to answer the question you set out, do we pursue money things? We don't. We haven't done that. We've pursued money survival things.

CM: Well, television was obviously an area that we thought could be lucrative and it was in some ways. And it helped us write some shows. Live shows. But we haven't been focussed on how to really market the work. We should have split the difference a bit.

SLH: When I first had my vision, I thought this group would be travelling all over the world doing our own original material…but I forgot to mention that we'd be rich in the vision.

RA: Many of the artists I've talked to also teach. And I'm assuming that some of you or all of you do teach. So the question is, when you teach, how does that inform your work?

SW: Teaching has always been a focus. We've always taught throughout our careers. I think you teach best what you need most to learn. So when you start getting on your feet teaching, it solidifies everything that you have been doing. It forces you to articulate what the hell you're doing. So I think every time I teach I feel stronger as a performer. And I feel stronger as an artist because I love seeing the spark in someone's eyes when you say, "If you just follow this premise, put yourself completely into it, you'll be amazed at what will come out of that." And I've seen students change right in front of me. There's nothing like it. I guess that would be the second most incredible high next to performing, working with students and seeing that twinkle.

RA: Is teaching formalized through your company?

SLH: We teach introductory mime and physical theatre and advanced theatre for actors who have had some physical theatre training. We also do mask-making and mask-wearing. Then we do senior improvisation for people who are involved in the theatre for them to just keep the wheels greased. We don't have an actual school, although it is something we've thought about.

RA: Have you actually considered creating a school?

SW: We've considered it. But we haven't done that yet. I am sure that will happen in the next few years.

MEM: We might set up something once a year on a regular basis in the summer. That's something we might do. But we don't have a building—right now we just have an office and a studio in downtown Halifax. We don't really have a school per se so that students from other countries could come and live here, you know. That's why we do our workshops in a way that can work with the facilities we have.

RA: But is this still an important part of the whole Jest in Time picture?

SW: Because of the technical overload of visual imagery and movies and television, I think this art form will become stronger as the years go on. I think that the art of mime and physical theatre will have a resurgence. I think people will be tired and they will begin to say, "I don't want to watch any more TV. I don't want to watch any more special effects. I actually want to see a human being. Take me somewhere."

SLH: I think that when Marcel Marceau created his Bip character, he helped mime in terms of visibility, but he also hurt the art form because the general public thinks that mime is only a little white-faced, striped-shirted guy in slippers making things that aren't real.

RA: Are you speaking about illusion mime?

SLH: Yes. What is important is the physical eloquence. Look at *Les Enfants du Paradis*, that famous movie; it is what mime is in its true essence. It's more in the essence of, the root of any theatre to begin with. It's because of mime that I can walk two miles right in front of you. I can climb a wall and at the same time I can show you all the emotional connection to sorrow, tragedy, anger, pathos, and I can show it to you in two feet without any special effects. And then film came along and wiped mime right out. There were mimes like Chaplin and Buster Keaton who tried to keep that going, then text came in and wiped it out. It's almost like we have to create a thing called "new mime."

CM: In terms of mime and physical theatre in Canada, our best experience in working in Canada has been in Quebec. We are an English Canadian company which has done two tours through Quebec: summer festivals in rural Quebec and the Just for Laughs Festival in Montreal.

RA: Is that because there's no language barrier?

CM: The appreciation of theatre is more deeply rooted and there is just much more of it.

SW: And they do know the art form of mime.

RA: Your new show celebrates fifteen years on the road as a troupe. Any future plans for new work?

SLH: We usually do a three-year plan. I don't care whether you think this is silly or not, but my long-term vision is that I've always wanted to perform in outer space. That's definitely one of my goals. I still want to accomplish that, with or without this company. I will go, even if I have to do it alone.

RA: You actually want to be the first actors in space?

SLH: Yes, space, the final frontier.

RA: Hey, that's something for the long-range planning. To wrap up and perhaps bring the conversation a little more earthbound, what do you think the hallmark of your company is?

SW: I would say adapting. Adapting.

CM: Energy.

SW: I'd say the adapting, the flexibility, and the ability to make people see things and enjoy themselves and laugh.

CM: Comedy, yeah.

MEM: Plus mirroring of life.

CM: Poignancy…and physical comedy. We want people to laugh.

RA: So there's satire and laughter?

SLH: When I think of what we have gone through to keep this company together—the sweat and blood and tears—it's been a remarkable achievement.

RA: What has taking your work out of your town and your province and then eventually out of your country done for you? Do you recommend it as a path for young artists? Should they be thinking about building the kind of work that can tour?

CM: Well, I think for me, being a new Canadian, it's been incredible to see every part of Canada. And I mean literally every small town in every province. And it's been incredible to be in front of the crowd and to figure out what it is to be a living, breathing performer. Not a hobby. Not something you do part-time.

SLH: So you're saying that the touring has been worth it, Christian?

CM: That's basically what I am saying. I mean, definitely, I've experienced magical moments. More than I would have, say, working at the bank.

MEM: And I think as young artists when you go out there and do all that touring, it feeds your work and you get exposed to different regions of Canada. And we've also done our international touring to different cultures. So that absolutely feeds into the work. So I recommend that for any young artist. I think staying here in this particular region you have to create your own work, so that also creates strength in you as an artist. You have to make it work here.

CM: When we started, there were very few companies down here. There are a lot more companies down here right now. Some of them are creation companies. Some of them are straight-ahead. We're developing Atlantic Canadian plays. But I think that has been a part of our legacy. We did it.

SLH: There was one thing I wanted to say when you asked us about our hallmarks. I think the imagination has power. That's important…without sounding too philosophical, I think that all great theatre is about becoming conscious.

RA: That's okay, in a book you can certainly become philosophical. Then twenty years down the line you'll say, "Oh, did I really say that?"

CM: When you're on Mars performing…

SLH: You just wait!

■ ■ ■

Trip, 2001. L-R: Mary Ellen MacLean, Sherry Lee Hunter, Shelley Wallace, Christian Murray. (Photo: Cylla von Tiedemann)

PRODUCTION HISTORY OF
JEST IN TIME THEATRE

2002 **Trip**
The Great Canadian Theatre Company, Ottawa

2002 **Peter and the Wolf**
With Symphony Nova Scotia, Halifax

2001 **Trip**
By Jest collective.
duMaurier Theatre, Halifax

2001 **Sleep Tracks and Handmade**
With Symphony Nova Scotia

2001 **Best of Jest and Sleep Tracks**
Tour of Japan

2000 **Fear**
By Andy Jones and Jest collective
Eastern Front Theatre

1999 **The Best of Jest**
duMaurier Theatre, Halifax

1999 **Love Bytes**
By Jest collective, Ed Macdonald, Carol Sinclair, Bette Macdonald, Bryden MacDonald, Catherine Banks, Mary Lou Martin, Christopher Shore, Joanne Miller, Geoff McBride, Mary-Colin Chisholm

1998 **Human Oddities**
By Jest.collective Directorial assistance by Ed MacDonald. duMaurier Theatre

1997 **Accidental Blood**
Co-created and directed by Bryden MacDonald

1996 **Jest in Time Meet Beckett**
International Beckett Festival
University of Victoria

1996 **Performance for Her Royal Majesty Queen Elizabeth II, Nova Scotia**

1992 **Jest in Time Meet Beckett**
Directed by Linda Moore. Neptune Theatre

1990 **Jesters Christmas**
By Jest collective. Neptune Theatre

1986-90 **Touring**
Since 1986 Jest has toured throughout Canada and the United States, as well as to Australia and Hong Kong

Neptune Productions

1997 **Seduced**
(Studio Series)

1992 **Alice**
(Main Stage)

2002 **Theatre Nova Scotia Robert Merritt Awards**
for Best Production and Best Director for *Trip.*

2002 **Theatre Nova Scotia Robert Merritt Award**
nominations for Best Production for *Handmade, Sleep Tracks, The Best of Jest, Trip.*

Handmade, 1991. L-R: Mary Ellen MacLean, Sherry Lee Hunter, Shelley Wallace, Christian Murray. (Photo: Cylla von Tiedemann)

LIST OF WORKS CITED

The Empty Space
By Peter Brook
London: Penguin Books, 1990

Mime: The Step Beyond Words
By Adrian Pecknold
Toronto: NC Press, 1982

The Moving Body: Teaching Creative Theatre
By Jacques Lecoq with Jean-Gabriel Carasso and Jean-Claude Lallias
Translated by David Bradby
London: Methuen Publishing Ltd., 2000

Theatre of the Oppressed
By Augusto Boal
Translated by Charles A. & Maria Odilia Leal McBride
London: Pluto Press, 1979

The Tricks of the Trade
By Dario Fo
Translated by Joe Farrell
London: Methuen Drama, 1991

COMPANY CONTACTS AND WEBSITES

Axis Theatre
Wayne Specht
Suite 203 -1398 Cartwright St
Vancouver, BC V6H 3R8
www.axistheatre.com

Theatre Beyond Words
Harro Maskow and Robin Patterson
P.O. Box 1690
Niagara-on-the-Lake, ON LOS 1J0
www.theatrebeyondwords.com

Ronnie Burkett
Rink-a-Dink Inc.
c/o John Lambert & Associates
3575 boulevard St-Laurent, # 110,
Montreal, QC H2X 2T7
www.johnlambert.ca

Theatre Columbus
Leah Cherniak and Martha Ross
174 Spadina Avenue, #510
Toronto, ON M5T 2C2
www.go7.ca

Yves Dagenais
c/o National Circus School
417 Berri Street
Montréal, QC H2Y 3E1
www.enc.qc.ca/ta-rens.html

Les Deux Mondes
Daniel Meillieur or Pierre MacDuff
7285 rue Chabot
Montreal, QC H2E 2K7
www.johnlambert.ca

Wendy Gorling
Studio 58, Langara College
100 W 49th Avenue
Vancouver, B.C. V5Y 2Z6
www.langara.bc.ca/studio58

Jest in Time
1585 Barrington Street
Halifax, NS B3J 1Z8
www.jestintime.ns.ca

Theatre Smith-Gilmour
Dean Gilmour and Michele Smith
174 Spadina Avenue, #510
Toronto, ON M5T 2C2
www.go7.ca

PHYSICAL THEATRE TRAINING PROGRAMMES

Canada

Studio 58
Langara College
Kathryn Shaw, Artistic Director
100 W 49th Avenue
Vancouver, BC
Canada V5Y 2Z6
www.langara.bc.ca/studio58

National Circus School
417 Berri Street
Montréal,QC
Canada H2Y 3E1
www.enc.qc.ca/ta-rens.html

L'Ecole de Mime Omnibus
3673, rue St. Dominique
Montréal, QC
H2X 2X8
www.mimeomnibus.qc.ca

Mime Theatre International
Guiseppe Condello
103-1070 Kings Road
Victoria, BC.
Canada V8T 1X1

USA

Dell'Arte International School of Physical Theatre
PO Box 816 T
Blue Lake, California, USA
www.dellarte.com

Celebration Barn Theater
Tony Montanaro
190 Stock Farm Road
South Paris, ME 04281
www.celebrationbarn.com

University of Connecticut
Department of Dramatic Arts
Bart Roccoberton, Director (Puppetry)
802 Bolton Road U - 1127
Storrs, CT- 06269-1127
puppetarts@finearts.sfa.uconn.edu

Europe

Desmond Jones School of Mime and Physical Theatre
20 Thornton Avenue
London W4 1QG, England

L'Ecole Jacques Lecoq
57, rue du Faubourg St. Denis
75010, Paris France
ecole-jacques-lecoq@wanadoo.fr

Ecole Philippe Gaulier
Paul Millican
PO Box 1815
London, England
N5 1BG

School of Physical Theatre
Ron East, Director
3 Mills Media Centre
Mills Lane
Bromly-by-Bow, London E3 3DU
England
www.physicaltheatre.com

Institut International de la Marionnette
Roman Paska, Director
(Puppetry-Object theatre)
7 place Winston Churchill 08000
Charleville - Meziers - France
www.marionnette.com

ROBERT ASTLE

Robert Astle is an Albertan by birth. In 1977, he went to Europe to study theatre, improvisation, acrobatics, and creation at the famed École Jacques Lecoq in Paris. He returned to Canada in 1979, and in 1982, he co-founded, with Jan Miller and Jan Henderson, Small Change Theatre, a theatre collective. He co-created, produced and performed in Small Change Theatre's internationally acclaimed clown and mask shows, which toured to festivals and theatres internationally.

In 1990, Robert returned to Europe to collaborate on the creation of his one-man show, *Heart of a Dog*, with Agnès Limbos. This collaboration resulted in the international theatre creation company "Les Établissements" which has toured his solo performance plays to festivals and theatres in Belgium, Canada, The United Kingdom, and the United States. Nuage Editions published it in 1994. In 2001, Astle adapted and recorded *Heart of a Dog* for CBC Radio's *Sunday Showcase*, which has been recently been nominated for the prestigious Prix Italia.

Robert Astle. (Photo: David Gow)

In 1996, Robert created his second solo show, *The Hats of Mr. Zenobe,* in collaboration with American artist, Jim Jackson, and Belgian writer and director, Agnès Limbos. The work had its premiere at Theatre Network in Edmonton, Alberta in 1997, and has played in Montreal, Toronto, Victoria, Colorado Springs, Whitehorse, and Calgary. In Toronto the production received four Dora Award nominations. Nuage Editions published the play in 1997. In the spring of 2002, Robert also performed in the new French translation *Les chapeaux de Monsieur Zenobe* in Montreal. Paul Lefebvre translated the play.

In 1998 Robert moved to Montreal and is currently teaching at the National Theatre School (Playwriting) and Concordia University, Department of Drama. Most recently, Robert has directed *Marie-Antoine, Opus 1* for Concordia University, and directed the Quebec premiere of the French author Michel Azama's play *Croisades* at Theatre Prospero. He was the co-producer of the Wildside Festival at the Centaur Theatre, where he was also serving as the playwright-in-residence for 2002-2003. His newest solo play, *The Piano Tuner*, will have its premiere in Montreal at the Centaur Theatre in January 2003. *Theatre Without Borders* is Robert's first non-fiction title.

AGMV Marquis
MEMBRE DE SCABRINI MEDIA
Québec, Canada
2002